FOCUS ON THE FAMILY®

love won out

How God's love

helped two people

leave homosexuality

and find each other

john&anne paulk

TYNDALE

Tyndale House Publishers, Wheaton, Illinois

Library of Congress Cataloging-in-Publication Data
  Paulk, Anne, 1963–
        Love won out / by Anne and John Paulk.
            p.   cm.
        ISBN 1-56179-783-9. — ISBN 1-56179-816-9
        1. Paulk, Anne, 1963–   . 2. Paulk, John. 3. Christian
  biography—United Stares.   4. Gays—United States Biography.
  5. Homosexuality—Religious aspects—Christianity.   6. Christian
  biography—United States. I. Paulk, John. II. Title.
  BR1725.P275A3   1999
  261.8'35566'0922—dc21   99-27731
  [B]   CIP

A Focus on the Family book published by Tyndale House Publishers,
Wheaton, Illinois.

People's names and certain details of their identities have been changed
to protect the privacy of the individuals involved. However, the events
have been conveyed with as much accuracy as possible.

Cover design: Shane Wagoner
Cover photo: Owen Carey

Printed in the United States of America

99 00 01 02 03 04/10 9 8 7 6 5 4 3 2 1

*To the thousands of men and women who have
had the courage to overcome homosexuality
in the face of a culture that says it's impossible,
we lovingly dedicate this book.*

∞

"Along unfamiliar paths I will guide them;
I will turn the darkness into light before them
and make the rough places smooth.
These are the things I will do;
I will not forsake them."

ISAIAH 42:16

Contents

⚬⚭⚬

Foreword

When it comes to homosexuality, I'm not proud of how we Christians have dealt with the subject or the people who struggle with it. I've been as guilty as any other Christian who has pointed a finger rather than putting an arm around someone who identified himself as gay, bisexual, or homosexual. I held it up as a sin worse than all others and thought I was better than anyone attracted to members of the same sex. My attitude changed, however, when I discovered that my brother was homosexual. For the first time, I realized there are real people behind this baffling thing called homosexuality.

From my experience with my brother, I came to understand that sexual identity struggles can't be explained away. The feelings of attraction are real and are based on unmet needs. Those needs are so strong that they compel a person toward the very thing that would repel most others. People don't wake up one morning and decide their lives would be better if they developed an attraction to members of the same sex; that attraction develops over time.

I believe the attraction starts young and is produced by one or a combination of situations. It can stem from many sources. One of those is rejection. Many gay men I've met tell stories of being outcasts early in life. They say they've been gay since birth, but in reality, they were *different*. They didn't like to do what most other boys did. Or they felt alone or abandoned. They longed to be accepted, but because they were more gentle, felt more deeply, or appreciated beauty more richly, their fathers and friends didn't really enjoy them. So they experienced profound rejection.

Others talk of being very social, but they longed for acceptance from a parent who was never there or was full of disdain for them. I've heard stories of fathers finding their young sons playing with dolls and picking up the dolls and demanding they never be touched again. It's too bad those fathers didn't pick up their sons and give them the touch they needed to feel complete.

With young homosexual women, I've found those same feelings of isolation and rejection. Because they didn't like what was defined as feminine or ladylike, they weren't accepted as real girls or refined young women. They weren't comfortable in stereotypical roles or play behaviors. They felt they had to forge their own way as outcasts, different from the rest.

Other things lead to same-sex attraction as well. At age five, my brother was molested by a young man in our church. This experience is all too common in the background of homosexuals. An early experience like that creates internal conflict and unnatural desires that aren't chosen but are imbedded by the sin of another. Often afraid to tell anyone or threatened with death if they do, these young people live with a secret that gains more power over them the longer they keep it hidden.

There's another common thread in the early development of many homosexuals, and you will read about it here in the life of John and Anne Paulk. It's the early exposure to pornography. Porn can create many reactions, but two that are common lay the foundation for homosexuality. One is to create a repulsion of the opposite sex out of fear or disgust. The other is to create a desire for someone of the same sex. The reaction varies based on the type of pornography, the messages that are presented with it, and the messenger who introduces the young person to it.

These are but a few of the complex situations that can occur in childhood and lead one into the world of homosexuality. None of them involves a choice on the part of the child; they're all the result of the sins of others. The issue of choice comes later in life, when a person decides what to do about the urges that have been created. Out in the world, the most common belief is that they must be sexualized—that it's okay to act on them and create a sexual relationship with someone of the same gender.

This is where the world and I part company. Those unmet needs and desires do not have to end up as homosexual behavior. Sadly, not many in our culture are telling struggling people that they don't have to act on their urges. Fortunately, that's changing.

When people make that first decision to engage in gay sex, it might be their last homosexual experience. They might conclude that gay sex is not a path they want to pursue. They might discover it didn't resolve all their internal conflicts or answer all their questions, so they move on. They then might explore other avenues to meet their needs, some healthy and some not so healthy.

For others, the first experience may lead to more. The sexual act might make them feel accepted, loved, and connected in a way they've longed for since childhood. Soon they may find themselves identifying more with other homosexuals than with heterosexuals. Eventually they may feel that it's only "normal" to live as they live and do what they do. The choice to explore leads them into total immersion in the gay world.

There's another choice that can be made, however—the choice to resolve the deep longings, the sexual confusion, the sense of rejection, and the desire for acceptance. It's a choice to heal the wounds of the past rather than sexualize them and develop a life that caters to the wounds. It's a decision to use the past to strengthen character rather than develop a world around the past. Every day, thousands of men and women make this choice and move beyond their early homosexual feelings.

Yet another choice—far more difficult—is the one you'll read about in the pages that follow. It's the decision of those who have already established their lives and identities around homosexuality to change—gradually and with much difficulty—from pursuing same-gender sex to pursuing God instead. I believe that when you pursue the God of the Bible, one day you'll discover that homosexual sex was not something He intended or desires for any of us. He warned us about it and wants to help anyone who is willing to move beyond it.

This choice to change doesn't mean that one minute all your desires are for someone of the same sex and the next minute they change forever and you're now attracted to the opposite sex. God could work such an instant transformation, but I've never met anyone who has had that experience. Instead, I know of people who make this tough decision, struggle with it, are tempted to abandon it, persevere, and then one day discover that the desires of their heart are starting to shift. Eventually they awake to the reality that they really are heterosexual. God uses the struggle to build character and draw them closer to Himself. This dramatic though difficult change is available to anyone who wants it.

Anne and John made that change. And they have stood up and without shame told the world about their pasts and how God healed them little by little, step by step. They're living evidence that change is possible and that sometimes that change results in connecting with the opposite sex, being attracted to a particular member of the opposite gender, and eventually a fulfilling marriage. All that is possible through the power of God and the determination of anyone who wants to follow Him. For others, however, the path may not be toward marriage but toward a life of fulfilled singleness. It could be a life of service to God that requires them to be single. *When we pursue God, we find to our amazement that we become more interested in what He wants than in what we think we need.*

In this wonderful book, you'll see honest feelings and honest struggles. The untidy parts have not been edited out. I like that, because God didn't edit them out of His Word, either. As you read this moving story by Anne and John, you'll discover real people with real hope for a future God has designed for them. If you're struggling with your sexual identity, I pray you'll recognize the truth here, truth that leads to hope. And I pray that you'll find courage to live the life God has designed for you.

If you don't struggle with your own sexual identity, I pray

you, too, will discover truth here—truth that will lead to compassion, understanding, and the same kind of deep love for homosexuals that Jesus has for them. If you're like me, you've said that you love the sinner but hate the sin. If you're really like me, however, you've really hated the sinner as well. Just admitting that is the first step toward healing your own brokenness. I pray you'll find healing yourself and that it will lead you to "be Jesus" to those who need to see Him and know Him as you do.

As Christians, we've too often been quick to judge those who are caught up in a world that's foreign to us. We can't understand why they insist on living the way they do. We've screamed the truth at them. I've even seen Christians hold up signs to inform them that "God Hates Fags." When I see all this, it's no mystery why homosexuals think Christians are cruel, uncaring, and more concerned about an agenda than a human being. Our world is foreign to them because often all they see is hate. Since they're looking for love (just like everyone), we've destroyed many opportunities to help them experience the love of the Lord whom we have so poorly represented.

When Jesus walked the earth, He was so attractive, so full of love and grace, that even the worst of the worst were drawn to Him. They responded to His love because, while He knew their sins, He also knew their hearts. He knew their sins were horrible, but also that the people behind the sins were His own unique creations.

Jesus suffers with struggling homosexuals and wants us to reach out to them and love them back to His plan for them. After you've read this story, I believe you'll be more motivated to do just that.

My thanks to John and Anne for their lives and their courage to share them with us all. Because of this story, I've grown in my understanding of homosexuality as a problem and as an opportunity for God's kingdom. John and Anne haven't encouraged us to give up our convictions of faith or even politics. Instead, they've challenged us to give up our pride and, where necessary, our hate. But more than anything else, they've given us an honest story of how God can change a soul and the desires of the heart. If you have ever wondered if it might be possible for you, read on. Herein lies proof of God's life-changing grace and love for you.

Stephen Arterburn
Founder of New Life Clinics
Author of many books, including How Will I Tell My Mother? *a book he wrote with his brother who died of AIDS in 1988*

Introduction: An Incredible Story

One gorgeous spring Sunday morning, as immense clouds drifted across a perfect Colorado sky, I (Anne) made my way from our church to our car. The service had been uplifting and encouraging, and now, as John and Timmy went ahead, I stopped to pick up a brochure. Walking toward the parking lot a minute later, I inhaled deeply, feeling glad to be alive and grateful for our new home, new church, and new life in Colorado Springs.

All at once, Sheryl, a new friend, rushed across the church patio. "Anne!" she cried. "There you are! It's so good to see you!" She hurried over to me in her characteristic out-of-breath way. "Are we still on for lunch tomorrow?"

We had moved to the city less than a month before, and meeting people was a top priority for John and me. I had met Sheryl at a weekly women's Bible study. She and I—both mothers of active two-year-olds—had decided to get baby-sitters and have lunch together on Monday at a great little restaurant that had just opened.

"Oh, Sheryl, I'm so sorry," I replied. "I was going to call you this afternoon if I didn't see you at church. I'm really disappointed, and I wish I didn't have to cancel, but John and I just got a call this morning, and we have to do an interview tomorrow at 11 A.M. It could take several hours."

"An interview?" she asked. "Really? Why are you and John being interviewed?"

I looked at Sheryl's puzzled expression and realized that if I didn't explain, she'd think I didn't want to go to lunch with her—and I really did. On the other hand, if I told her the whole story, we'd be standing there for a long time.

"So what will you be interviewed about?" she persisted.

I took a deep breath. "Oh, it's a very long story." I paused, wondering where to begin. "Sometimes we're interviewed about our lives and about our decision to follow Christ out of a challenging past. I'll have to tell you all about it when we have lunch."

"Really? That's awesome! But where will your interview be? Can I watch it or read about it?"

"Yes, eventually you'll be able to. It's a cover story for *Newsweek*, and it'll be out this summer."

"*Newsweek*?" Sheryl's eyes widened in surprise. "That's a major magazine! Why on earth is *Newsweek* interviewing you and John for a cover story?"

I laughed. "Like I said, it's a long story. But for now, I'll give you a synopsis. You see, with the help of Christ, John and I both came out of homosexuality. Eventually we fell in love and married. My face and my story were just featured in a full-page ad in the *New York Times*, and now our phone line is being inundated with requests for interviews."

Sheryl's face was a study in astonishment. "Anne, I had no idea about any of this! I didn't even know people *could* come out of homosexuality!"

"Well, they can—John and I did, with God's help. But a lot of media types don't even believe people like John and I exist. Anyway, it's important for us to share our story. So I'm afraid I'll have to cancel and reschedule our lunch for another day. I'm so sorry, Sheryl. I hope you understand."

Sheryl gave me a quick hug and a big smile. "Of course I understand. But wow, Anne, what an incredible story! I can't wait to hear all about it!"

I walked thoughtfully across the parking lot, enjoying the fresh breeze and the brilliant sunlight. "One of these days, we're going to have to write a book about our lives," I told John as I joined him and Timmy in the car.

John nodded. "I know," he responded. "I've been thinking the same thing."

"What would we call it?" I asked, my mind struggling to imagine a book cover with our names on it.

John was quiet for a few moments before he replied, "You know, I think I'd like to call it *Love Won Out*, because in spite of everything, in the face of all the odds, God's love found a way."

"*Love Won Out*," I repeated. "You're right, John. That really is what happened to us, isn't it?"

"Yes, by God's grace that's what happened. That's exactly what our story is all about."

Child's Play

Anne
⌒⌒

John and I have been photographed, interviewed, and seen on television together for years. But even before we met, and long before our marriage became the subject of both curiosity and controversy, our young lives ran on parallel tracks in a number of different ways. We were both born in 1963, both graduated from high school in June 1981, and both became seriously involved in homosexuality during college.

Our experiences were unique in some respects but nearly identical in others. Both of us became Christian believers while still entangled in homosexuality. We finally met in the late 1980s at an Exodus International ministry called Love in Action. John was one year ahead of me in the residential program when we were introduced.

But I'm getting ahead of myself. Let's start at the beginning.

I was born in Lewiston, Idaho, the youngest child by nearly six years, almost my own generation within my family. My parents were genuinely excited about my arrival, as were my brothers and sister. Our family was, at least on the surface, quite ordinary.

John's arrival was less "convenient." In 1962, his parents were college students who were dating. Once his mother realized she was pregnant, she and his father got married. John was born in Springfield, Illinois.

From early childhood until I was four years old, I was as normal as could be. I played with dolls, tried to look pretty, and wanted to be a feminine little girl. I wore cute dresses and took ballet and tap lessons. I remember coveting the pink tutus my friend wore to our dancing classes. I was a secure, comfortable, and happy child who, like most girls my age, played with Barbies.

One of the few unhappy experiences I recall from my earliest years involved my efforts to stop wetting the bed. I couldn't have been more than three years old at the time, and I remember being very proud of myself that night, tiptoeing to the bathroom and using the toilet while everyone else slept. All at once, as I climbed back into bed, my father's figure loomed in my bedroom doorway.

"What's all the racket?" he demanded.

I was terrified. "What racket, Daddy?" I asked.

"You flushed the toilet and woke me up!" he growled. "Don't you realize I have to go to work tomorrow? I need my sleep!"

"I'm sorry, Daddy," I said, beginning to cry. "I was trying not to wet the bed."

"Don't let it happen again," he warned. Then he turned and walked away, leaving me feeling guilty and ashamed.

Unfortunately, that incident wasn't the worst thing that would happen to me in childhood. John and I both endured some troublesome and unpleasant experiences at around the age of four that would eventually lead us in the same direction.

John Darrell was tall and thin, with a mop of blond hair. He was about 14 years old and I was four when he came to our apartment to baby-sit while my parents went out to dinner. I still remember him fairly well.

Darrell and I had a great time at first, listening to music and dancing around the living room. As kids do, we were soon jumping on the bed and being a little more rowdy than my parents might have wanted. Then, all at once, Darrell said, "Do you want to see something neat?"

Of course I answered, "Yeah, yeah! What is it?"

Instead of showing me something wholesome or worthwhile, Darrell unzipped his pants and exposed himself to me. I remember staring at him and wondering, *Why is he showing me that?*

He made a little game of it—I was supposed to show myself to him, too. He was sexually aroused, and though he didn't touch me, it was my first exposure to male nudity. My dad had always been very modest, and I don't have any memories of taking showers or baths with him.

Darrell wasn't the least bit modest, however, and even as a small child I was kind of intrigued. His behavior didn't scare me or cause me to want to run away. Instead, I was more or less transfixed by what he was doing.

"Now, John," Darrell told me once he was dressed and ready to leave, "don't you dare tell your parents or anyone about our little game. Understand?"

I nodded mutely, dazed by the experience. I liked Darrell, and I didn't want to get him—or myself—in trouble. I never told a soul.

I don't recall whether Darrell baby-sat for our family again, but his memory and that uninvited introduction to male sexuality were firmly implanted in my mind. As the days and weeks passed, my thoughts continually wandered back to the image of Darrell's naked body. He was a fully developed teenager, and his masculinity tugged on my imagination like a magnet. I was excited that this guy had taken an unusual interest in me, and I was fascinated by what I had seen.

Meanwhile, at just about the same time, Anne had her own introduction to male sexuality through another 14-year-old boy.

Anne

"Won't it ever stop raining?" I asked my sister impatiently as I looked out the water-streaked window of our house that fateful afternoon.

It was a gray, cloudy day, and every kid in our neighborhood was bored and restless. We ended up going from one house to the next, looking for things to do. I was about four at the time, and I was in the bedroom of a 14-year-old boy, rummaging under his bed for a tennis ball we'd been bouncing off a wall. His bed was unmade, and I noticed something sticking out from under the mattress. Ever curious, I yanked it out, stared at it for a moment, and caught my breath. In my hands was a magazine featuring page after page of nude women who were exposing themselves in the most shocking ways.

Several magazines were hidden there, and I managed to look at two or three before I heard my sister saying, "Anne! Where are you?" Feeling panicked, I stuffed everything back under the mattress and fled the room.

I thought a lot about those pictures over the next few days. I wasn't so sure the boy's stash of magazines was a good idea. I even considered asking my parents, "Is it all right for him to look at those pictures?"

It's too bad I never asked the question. Instead, the boy's sister and I began to look at the photographs ourselves. One day I remarked to him, "Are you sure you should be looking at these things? And how come there aren't any pictures of boys in here?"

I guess that created an opportunity for him to say, "Oh, really? Well, let me show you something ..."

The episode that followed didn't involve sexual intercourse, but as the boy and I played a sort of hide-and-seek game with a flashlight, he made sure it touched his genitals. I remember wondering why he kept placing the object where I had to find it in the same place again and again. I became bored with the game long before he did. I didn't understand sexual arousal and had no idea he was using me for his own ends.

Although I'm sure the young man's intention was to stimulate himself, I also think he wanted to keep me from spreading the word about his pornography. Regardless, I felt dirtied and ashamed immediately afterward.

The boy warned me, "Don't tell anybody! We're going to get in big trouble if you do!"

And of course, I believed him.

My lips were sealed. I didn't understand what had just happened, but I did understand, somewhere deep in my heart, that

I had participated in something very wrong. I felt vulnerable, unprotected, and exposed, and I had no one to explain what had just happened to me. I felt very much like what I imagine Adam and Eve must have felt in the garden of Eden—naked and afraid.

Why didn't I tell my parents? Looking back, I know they cared for us kids with the best intentions and the highest standards for themselves and us. But they also seemed to have the expectation that everything that took place within our family would be perfect, without the possibility of wrongdoing. I don't think they understood brokenness or moral imperfection. Perhaps that's why they seemed unapproachable, unable to cope with "bad things."

I can still see my mother, her brown hair shiny and neat, her body fit and trim because of her continuous activity. She was always busy with cleaning, cooking, and chasing after her children. The greatest demand in her life was keeping up with the challenges of raising two not-so-perfect teenage boys.

Dad was lean, athletic, analytical, and handsome. We must have looked like the Cleaver family in some respects. Dad was both preoccupied and exhausted by his work. And he, too, struggled with the behavior management of his sons, finding a certain amount of solace in golf. Dad wasn't particularly involved with us beyond athletics, routine activities around the house, and corrections of our behavior. Above all, he was emotionally absent a great deal of the time. He would get so focused on TV or household projects that he wouldn't hear you even if you called his name several times. I've always been amazed by his ability to completely tune out other people.

Whether I'd been four or 14, the thought of reporting to either Mom or Dad a personal incident involving pornography and molestation was about as unlikely as anything I could imagine.

Instead of talking about it, in the days and weeks that followed my experience with the neighbor boy, I kept wanting to hide. It was a strange feeling—I'd never felt so vulnerable and insecure. I started having recurring dreams and strange night-mares. At about the same time, being ever so helpful, my 10-year-old sister announced, "If you dream the same dream three times, it's going to come true." I was soon convinced that the scary dreams of tigers invading our family and attacking my mom and dad were definitely going to come true—my big sister had said so, hadn't she? I was more frightened than I realized.

To the core of my being, I felt powerless and defenseless. I sensed there was nothing I could do to prevent such a sexual trespass from happening again. I didn't dare talk to anyone about it. Instead, I just closed off emotionally and subconsciously put up barriers against ever feeling so unsafe again.

In retrospect, I think that somehow, in my sensitive, young mind, I equated the fact that I was a girl with the act of being violated. That explains why it wasn't long before I began to reject my female qualities. My outward looks changed radically, a reflection of what was going on inside. For example, I suddenly refused to wear dresses. My behavior also began to change dramatically. Almost overnight, I rejected everything that had to do with femininity—games, dolls, and all. I started playing cops and robbers and cowboys and Indians with neighborhood boys my age.

Being a girl made me vulnerable and weak, and I didn't like being a little girl anymore.

Meanwhile, another unexpected event shook my world—my beloved grandpa died. Looking back years later, my mother remarked, "Oh, yes, I did see something change in you, but I thought it was grief over the loss of your grandfather."

My mother was right, but only in part. I had been very close to Grandpa. My sister and I would vie for the position of sitting closest to him on our stairwell. We both felt safe and protected by him, and I knew beyond a doubt that he really loved me and adored me as his "special little girl." At the time, I didn't understand that he had reinforced my femininity, but that's exactly what he had always done. And now he was gone.

At about this same time, in what seemed like an unrelated incident, I asked a neighbor boy to pull his pants down. The event wasn't much of a secret—it happened right out on the sidewalk. I was more curious than anything else, but when his parents heard what I had asked him to do, they wouldn't allow him to be around me anymore. His mother and father were horrified and shamed him unmercifully. And when the story came out, I was overwhelmed with disgrace.

John

⊗

"My gosh!" I gasped. "Check this out!"

"What is it?" my friend asked, his eyes widening at the sight of a full-page photograph of a naked woman.

I was five or six years old at the time, and like Anne and most kids, I was sexually curious. That day, while a friend and I were walking along beside the river, something had caught my eye. I'd walked over and picked up the colorful magazine, its pages fluttering in the breeze.

"Wow!" my friend exclaimed, tugging the magazine out of my hands. "Whose do you think it is?"

We looked at each other, then glanced around nervously, suddenly afraid of being caught. "I don't know, but let's get out of here!" I said breathlessly, hiding the magazine under my shirt. We both headed for home, running as fast as we could.

Once we felt safe, we sat in some bushes and looked at the magazine again. It was hardcore pornography. The photos of women were shocking. I had never seen women in positions like that before, and the sight of them horrified me. To my young eyes, it looked as if they were being tortured. However, although I was afraid and troubled, I couldn't tear myself away.

That first exposure to pornography proved to be a devastating experience in more ways than one. It began to create in me an ambivalence toward women. My dependence on my mother was an ever-increasing fact of my life, yet the female exploitation I had seen troubled me at a deep level. The strange, abnormal depiction of females began to repel me from female sexuality. It also planted an ugly seed in my mind—a seed of fascination with pornography.

Anne Jesse was an adorable little boy. I can still remember his black hair and big, dark eyes. All the other girls in our kindergarten class had crushes on him, but he paid the most attention to me. One day we were talking to each other and he complained, "I've got a headache."

I smiled and said, "My dad gets headaches, too. I know what to do." Then I began to rub Jesse's shoulders. He was happy to let me continue, but our teachers weren't the least bit pleased.

"Anne! Get your hands off Jesse this minute!" Miss Chambers yelled. "That is inappropriate touching!"

My face burned with embarrassment. I tried to explain, "But he said he had a headache, and—"

"Don't talk back to me, Anne!" Miss Chambers interrupted. "You come and sit over here right now!"

For some reason I'll never understand, both my kindergarten teachers were infuriated with me. They reacted to that innocent back rub as if I had done something terrible. They pulled me aside, scolded me, and punished me.

Worse, they told my parents about it.

That night, Mom looked at Dad as if to ask, "What shall we do?" She had no idea how to respond to the situation.

I watched my father sadly, longing for him to take me in his arms and tell me it wasn't my fault and everything was going to be all right. But he didn't do a thing. Instead, he walked out of the room and, in his characteristically detached way, simply clicked on the television.

Once again, I was deeply shamed. Once again, being a little girl who likes boys had proved to be dangerous and humiliating.

John

⌒∞⌒

"Kids," my dad began, "there's something I have to tell you. This is very hard for me, but ..."

I was seven years old and had been enjoying a day at the park with my father and sister. But now Dad was on his knees, facing Vicky and me and trying to tell us something. I was shocked to see he was having a hard time controlling his emotions. His face was sorrowful and his voice broke, and soon he was crying so hard that he could barely speak.

"I'm not going to be living with you anymore," he continued. "Your mother and I are getting a divorce."

Divorce! The subject had never before crossed my mind. Yet suddenly, without warning, I was facing an unknown future. I felt both terrified and heartsick. And when the day quickly arrived for Dad to actually leave us, I could hardly control my tears. But that was only the beginning of disturbing changes in my young world.

Before long, another man began to visit our apartment. Sometimes I found his clothes in the closet. And sometimes, late at night, I heard strange sounds coming from the living room.

One night as I lay in my bed, listening, my heart started pounding too fast and too hard. Something was wrong! What could I do? Shaking with fear, I gathered all my courage and decided to investigate.

When I walked downstairs, I found my mother and her friend Todd locked in an intimate embrace on the couch. Before I could ask what they were doing, Todd became enraged. He leapt up and shouted, "Get out of here, you little ___," chasing me out of the room.

Terrified, I ran back to my bed, sobbing and shaken. Todd was hurting my mother—I was sure of it! I crawled under my blankets and cried my eyes out, powerless to help her. I hated Todd for what he was doing.

The next morning, I tried to explain to Mom what I thought. "Todd was hurting you last night," I began.

"Mind your own business, John!" she snapped, not impressed by my concerns.

Todd moved in with us shortly thereafter.

Todd wanted to become my pal, but I had hated him ever since that night when I had interrupted his intimacy with my mom, thinking he was hurting her. I never forgave him for that. Besides, he and Mom came from very different social classes, and I felt he wasn't good enough for her and just didn't fit into our family. I never gave him a break.

At the same time, I felt highly protective toward Mom. In my young mind, I was convinced that Todd had been hurting her. It was up to me to keep safe this beautiful lady whom I idolized and imitated in many ways, even when her occasional angry words made me wonder just how much she loved me.

Life at home was becoming more unpredictable for me, but I could count on getting together with my dad on the weekends. We did a lot of fun things—going to the park, seeing a movie. But no matter how hard I tried, nothing I did seemed to please Dad.

One afternoon, my sister and Dad and I were at the park. "Why don't you and Vicky climb up the monkey bars?" he suggested. "Let's see who can get to the top first."

Dad knew well that I wasn't going to make it to the top, but he never stopped hoping I would develop some athletic skills.

"C'mon, John, you can do it!" he encouraged. "Just put one hand over the other and lift yourself."

I was terrified. But I wanted so much to overcome my fear that I extended my arms, gripped the bars with white knuckles, and pulled as hard as I could. My effort was short-lived. As always, once I got about two feet into the air, I panicked and started to cry.

"I ... I can't, Dad," I sniffled.

He simply turned and walked off in anger.

Things weren't any better at his home. I was constantly spilling my milk on the table, dropping food on the floor, or breaking a glass or a plate. "John! Will you watch what you're doing?" he'd shout. Dad's frustration with me was palpable.

I felt clumsy and inadequate. I was too uncoordinated, too frail, and too talkative. No matter what I tried to tell him, he never seemed to be listening. And the older I got, the more he distanced himself from me. Dad hardly ever complimented me, and when I was with him, I always felt like a failure and a reject. Still, I yearned for his approval.

After Dad remarried, in the only way I knew, I tried to get closer to him. One day, I courageously asked if I could live with him and his new wife, Ellen. It wasn't an easy question for me to ask as a nine-year-old, and the answer I received was shattering.

"No, John, it just wouldn't work," he responded bluntly and without so much as a moment's consideration. Then, just to make sure I caught on, he said it again: "No, I don't think your living with us would be a good idea at all."

Anne

While John was feeling unworthy as a little boy, I was becoming more and more of a tomboy.

"Anne, look at what I bought you!" my mother would say, pulling what I thought was the ugliest dress in the world out of a shopping bag.

"Ick! I hate lace, Mom," I'd reply. "I like wearing jeans and T-shirts, not dresses. Especially not dresses like *that*."

Mom was an attractive woman who styled her hair and wore makeup, but she didn't teach my sister, Paula, or me those skills, nor did she help me see what kind of clothes would flatter me or train me in how little girls should (and shouldn't) look. And, of course, I had my own deep-seated reasons for rejecting "girl stuff."

I was quiet and terminally shy, afraid of failure, and in my
early years I wouldn't even communicate with aunts and uncles
in English. Instead, I spoke a made-up, "imaginary" language. I
really wanted to please special adults, but I was afraid to take
risks. Those qualities helped lock me in my prison of silence following the sexual incident at age four. They also caused me to
struggle with the social demands of school.

Since I didn't think I belonged with the other kids, I was
reluctant to participate in recess activities. I felt unwelcome in
their games and excluded from their conversations. In the
meantime, as weeks and months went by, I was becoming
increasingly masculine-looking. I didn't look anything like the
little girl I'd once been. I didn't look like a boy yet, either, but I
was getting there.

For one thing, my haircuts were disastrous. For another, I
had to wear glasses. As a result, I was scared and socially inept,
and during recess and lunch I longed to go back to class, even
though I didn't enjoy schoolwork either.

Eventually I made friends with another third-grader named
Carolyn. Maybe she felt left out, too. But at last I had someone
to spend time with during recess. Even better, we began to play
together outside of school. Our families soon got to know one
another a little, which gave us lots of opportunities to be
together.

One day Carolyn suggested, "Hey Anne, let's pretend that
we're each other's boyfriends!"

"What do you mean?" I asked.

"You know, like you can be Donny Osmond, and I'll be your
girlfriend."

We were both hooked on teen magazines, and we adored
Donny Osmond, one of our many male "idols."

"So what do we do?" I asked, fascinated by the idea.

She answered enthusiastically, "We can just act like a
boyfriend and a girlfriend. You know, we could hold hands, hug
and kiss, and other stuff like that."

I accepted my male role eagerly and found that I really enjoyed it. Pretending to be a boy was satisfying, because I was able to take the initiative as boys are supposed do. Essentially, it put me in control.

Before long in this pretend game we were playing, Carolyn and I began to kiss each other. That meant I had her attention in a very special way. I felt safe, warm, and intimate with her. I looked forward to kissing her more and more. Now, in retrospect, if you analyze the game we were playing, I was rejecting myself and pretending to become someone else. My true needs weren't being met at all. My world was being turned upside down in imagination. But I was incapable of such analysis at the time; I simply relished my newfound feelings of affection and belonging.

John

"Oh yeah, I'm sure Todd has *Playboy* magazines," I said excitedly. I rushed around the apartment, looking for them, not having a clue about what I was looking for.

I was around nine years old, and by then my mother had married Todd, so he had become my stepfather. The two boys who were supposed to be taking care of Vicky and me had asked if Todd had any *Playboy* magazines. At the time, I didn't know what a *Playboy* magazine was, but I wanted to impress them.

One of the teenagers said, "Let's go look in your stepdad's bedroom." So we began to search through Todd's closet, and we soon found far more than Playboy magazines. There were stacks and stacks of hard-core magazines. Since I was already interested in pornography, this was quite a discovery.

I found myself being drawn back to that pornography again and again. At about that time, *Penthouse* had started publishing pictures of men and women together. And for some reason, I found myself attracted to the scenes where men were involved.

If only a woman's body was exposed, I wasn't all that interested. But when nude male bodies were revealed, I couldn't keep my eyes off them.

Anne Like John, I was also becoming addicted to
~~~~~~   pornography, though in my case it was a brother
          who had a stash in his room.

In a way, it seems odd that I wasn't completely repulsed by porn, considering what had happened to me at age four. But that incident apparently had the opposite effect, because at eight or nine years old, I would repeatedly sneak into my brother's room to read the strange stories and peer at the sexually explicit photographs in his magazines. I knew exactly where he kept them and precisely what they looked like. I learned to pull out one magazine at a time and then replace it exactly where it was before, shut the doors just as they had been, and leave his room unseen. No one ever knew I'd been in there.

I don't remember being aroused by looking at the women— at least not at first. I was simply fascinated by their bodies. I remember comparing myself to the models and feeling I was nothing in comparison. My brother's pornography was soft-core, but it was powerfully addictive.

After school got out in 1972, our family left Idaho. Our new Pennsylvania neighborhood was beautiful in a "Father Knows Best" way, and our house was bigger and more tasteful than anything we'd lived in before. Graceful trees lined the streets, and by the time our family unpacked and got settled in mid-June, roses were blooming everywhere. One grassy lawn spilled onto the next, and in the evenings we played outside until the fireflies appeared and the old-fashioned streetlights came on, casting a soft glow across well-tended gardens.

We found that the East Coast was more affluent than Idaho, with a greater focus on the arts. The population was more diverse and better educated. My family all began to attend the local Presbyterian church, and our life together was stable. My older brother was no longer living with us, however; he had started hitchhiking around the country like many other '70s kids. Month after month, more children moved into our neighborhood, and some of them became new friends of mine. I didn't mind this starting over except for one little problem: I felt homesick for Carolyn.

John It was Todd's big idea—which caused me to hate him more than ever—that I should join a Little League team. The best part of being involved in Little League was getting to wear the Padres' uniform, because most of the time I was either bored or embarrassed.

I was always getting stuck over in right field where the daisies grew. I'd stand there for hours, and no balls would ever come to me. I would pray, *Please, God, don't let anybody hit a ball this way, because if they do, I'll never catch it.*

By far, however, the most terrifying aspect of Little League was being up at bat. The crowd would yell, "Hey, batter, batter, batter," and I would always strike out. Not once did I ever hit a pitch. This never-ending failure was incredibly humiliating, especially when I was called a girl, a sissy, or a fag by the people in the stands.

I remember staring into the mirror at home, thinking about the names I had been called. *Am I really a sissy?* I'd ask myself, studying my reflection. *Do I really look like a girl?* The small, sad face that stared back at me was tear-streaked and puzzled. I had no one to answer my questions. Todd was the last person I'd turn to for advice, and I was fairly sure my mother wouldn't really understand my confusion.

I think things might have gone differently if I could have run into my dad's arms when I was rejected, if he had helped me learn skills to deal with the abuse, and if he had taken me out after school and taught me how to play ball. Maybe my confidence as a boy would have developed more normally and my sexuality would have been less confusing. Instead, playing Little League baseball was—to say the least—one of the most embarrassing things that ever happened to me. If boys had to play baseball, I didn't like being a boy.

Anne   Laurie, who was a year younger than me, moved
 ⟨✑⟩   into a house down the street about a year after my
         family arrived in Pennsylvania. I was now about 10, and while she seemed secure and content as a little girl, I continued to look and act boyish. But somehow the two of us got into the kissing game I had played with Carolyn. Only in this case, it was less of a role-playing game and more of a sensual experience. In fact, Laurie began to touch me sexually. Up until that time, I'd had no idea there was anything to do "down there."

I felt squeamish about our activities, and I was pretty sure we shouldn't be doing what we were doing. Then one day, Laurie's mother came in and caught us in the act. Once again, I was deeply shamed, primarily because her mother blamed me for the entire incident.

Laurie's mother ordered me to get out and go home, and she indignantly reported to my mother what had taken place between the two of us. When Mom questioned me, I explained that I felt kind of strange about the whole thing and that Laurie had come up with the idea. Thankfully, Mom believed me. And, since I was telling the truth, her response was a good and healthy one. I've always wondered where Laurie learned that kind of behavior. Someone older and more experienced must have introduced her to it.

Later that year, my friend Carolyn moved to New York. It was a substantial drive away, but because our families were friends, we got together now and then. Carolyn and I quickly resumed our little kissing game. By now we were both becoming more mature, and her interest was definitely toward boys.

But in our imaginary game, her allure was acted out toward me. So I was attracted to her as a lesbian, and she was attracted to me by pretending I was a boy. It was a sad form of intimacy, but although it was unsatisfying, it was intensely addictive.

That summer, our family drove up and down the East Coast. We traveled to New York City, for instance, where we saw our first Broadway play and watched the Radio City Music Hall Rockettes perform.

As we visited various points of interest, I became aware that people couldn't tell I was a girl. My grooming, posture, clothing, and hairstyle all gave them the impression, from a distance, that I was a boy. I found this absolutely humiliating.

One day I walked out of a gas station restroom and a tough-looking woman was standing outside, waiting her turn. "Can't you read?" she demanded. "It says 'women'!"

I stared at her and protested, "But I'm a girl!"

"Sure you are!" she scoffed, stomping out a cigarette. "You're a girl and I'm a boy. Next time, just use the men's room, okay?"

Tears burned my eyes, and I flushed red with shame. It had never been my conscious intention to look like a boy, although I think my rejection of femininity was a subconscious decision that began at the age of four or five. My masculine style was simply a cover-up for my feelings—a thick, impenetrable barrier to protect myself. And the older I got, the more pronounced my gender confusion became. My physical appearance, however, was hurting me far more than protecting me.

John

"John, either stop talking or go stand outside until you think you can be quiet!" my teacher ordered.

"I wasn't talking!" I insisted. "It was Joey."

Joey sat next to me, and he was the quietest kid in the entire school. Never once had he opened his mouth to speak—not even at recess. Everyone knew he wasn't about to interrupt while the teacher was talking, so the whole class started laughing uproariously.

"Joey hasn't said a word, John, and you know that very well," she challenged. "Believe me, I recognize your voice when I hear it."

"No, Mrs. Claypool," I persisted, "you really need to keep an eye on Joey. He talks more than you think he does."

Mrs. Claypool's face was darkening with rage. "John, go stand outside the classroom *this instant*. And if you say another word, you're going straight to the principal's office!"

By the fourth grade, I was always getting in trouble at school. I'd talk out of turn and try to make classmates laugh; I couldn't sit still; I was always leaving my desk; I verbally abused a student teacher for being Jewish. These behaviors led my teacher to think I might have emotional problems, so she sent me to the staff psychologist. He, in turn, sent me on to Children's Hospital, where tests showed that I had dyslexia, had a hard time concentrating, and was emotionally unstable because of my mother and stepfather's marriage. To calm me down, they started giving me Ritalin.

The school therapist, a tall, gentle man, had seemed genuinely interested in me. When he sent me on after only a couple of visits, I was devastated. "Please don't leave me!" I imagined myself pleading with him. "I want you to take me home and be my dad!"

Meanwhile, I was painfully aware that I didn't fit in with most of the other boys. A kid named Trevor was constantly taunted and teased, especially on the playground, for being effeminate, and I recognized how similar I was to him. "Nellie!" the boys would yell at him derisively, among other things. One day I got sick to my stomach as I thought about how much alike we were.

When it came to my fellow boys, I felt as if I were always on the outside, looking into their world.

With girls, on the other hand, I felt safe. So I played hopscotch and foursquare with them and tried to get involved in their conversations. One time, in an attempt to make myself feel important, I tried to play junior counselor to a girl and her boyfriend. Another time, trying to score points with my whole fourth-grade class, I brought in some chocolate-covered marshmallow cookies as a treat. One boy smashed his with his fist to see the filling go flying out, and immediately it seemed that everyone was doing the same thing. They were having a good time, but I felt humiliated. Once again I was made fun of; I was different. I just didn't fit in, especially with the boys.

Anne
⚬∞⚬

"Hey, you want to play spin the bottle with us?" I was on my feet, ready to go, before I thought twice.

The year was 1974, and my sister and I were baby-sitting for a neighborhood family. When the kids started playing spin the bottle, my adrenaline surged.

These kids were a disreputable group whose parents didn't seem to care what they did, but I wanted desperately to fit in. So once I found out they were playing spin the bottle, I was prepared to expose my body and even lose my virginity—anything to "belong" in their wild, little crowd.

Fortunately, my sister stopped me. With great wisdom she told me, "Anne, don't do it! It's not worth it." She talked me out of it, at least for the time being.

My sister, Paula, was five and a half years my elder, though she always bragged about being six years older. She was slender, but she always beat me in wrestling because she was bony and her elbows were sharp. She had straight, black hair, an outgoing personality, and a total lack of fear about speaking her mind. In this case, it was a good thing she did.

I hadn't even gone through puberty, yet I was already trying to seize control of my sexuality. *If I could get rid of my virginity, I told myself, I wouldn't have to deal with these feelings of shame any-*

more. Admittedly, it doesn't make much sense now, but somehow it sounded reasonable then.

That summer, our family moved again, this time to Walnut Creek, California. During my first months there, I enjoyed healthy and wholesome relationships. I made new friends, had a wonderful teacher, and began to enjoy myself. In short, I started with a clean slate.

John

My relationship with my mother was a puzzle. I loved her deeply and dearly, yet our relationship was complex and infuriating.

I was well aware that she was extremely controlling. For example, no matter what we talked about, no matter how much I was hurting, and no matter how much I needed her understanding and help, within minutes she inevitably turned any conversation back to herself.

"John, I'm so sorry the kids at school are making fun of you," she would say, "and I wish I could help. It's just like what always happens to me …"

Off she would go, talking about her life, her problems, and her needs.

One time, for example, a kid named Mark had threatened to beat me up, so I hid in a classroom for an hour and a half after school to avoid him. When I got home, I was crying and feeling incredibly lonely and picked on. I crawled into Mom's lap and started telling her how bad I felt.

Within two minutes, trying to relate, she began recounting her own troubled childhood. For the next hour, she went on and on about how miserable and unhappy she was, how hard her mother had been on her, and how isolated she had felt as a child. I soon tuned her out, trying to think of anything but what she was saying. By the end of the conversation, I and my problem had "disappeared," and I was putting my arm around her shoulder and consoling her.

I hated her every time that happened, yet I felt I couldn't survive without her approval.

Between my mother's drinking and her husband, Todd, she had more than her share of difficulties. Meanwhile, I was battling learning disabilities, gender confusion, and social rejection. I had little to offer my mother but love. And, if anything, I loved her too much.

Anne

꩜

"Mom, I'm so embarrassed...." I began.

My mother studied me closely. She was perplexed by my obvious distress. "Well, it's really not so bad," she tried to console. "You can always wear a hat."

Those words were the last thing I wanted to hear. Would she ever understand my needs or my problems?

"Wear a hat? For two months, Mom?" I complained. "My hair is only an inch long all the way around!" My words poured out in torrents of frustration. "I have to start junior high school in a month, and I look so horrible! I can't let my new classmates see me like this. I look like a boy! I'll be humiliated!"

I had naively trusted a hairdresser to cut my hair in a new style, giving her permission to do whatever she wanted, hoping for a more feminine and flattering style. I'd envisioned a look that was cute and attractive, something I could actually take care of myself. Instead, before I realized what was happening, the stylist had practically shaved my head. I looked more like a boy than ever.

I was mortified. And as much as I resented my mother's blasé suggestion, I wore a hat for at least a month. I took it off only when I had to—during class.

Maybe no one will notice me, I told myself on the first day of school. And in a way I was right. To the cool, popular girls, I was invisible. Only the loudmouth mockers seemed to see me, and naturally, they made themselves heard.

"Hey, Butch!" one of them called. "Don't you ever get tired of looking like one of the guys?"

An eighth-grade boy made his remarks in the cafeteria, and I fought off tears the rest of the day.

As I made my way home that afternoon, my sense of despair was acute. The same thoughts spun around and around in my mind: *You're not good enough. You don't have what it takes. You'll never be accepted, no matter how hard you try.*

Adolescent Encounters

John

"John, you're becoming more like your mother every day!"

Dad and I were driving to a movie one Saturday when he began sharing his views about my relationship with my mother. "It's no wonder you're so much alike. You're way too close to her emotionally, and to be honest, you act just like her, both in your mannerisms and your speech patterns."

I was shattered once again. The more I thought about what he had said, the worse I felt. I was humiliated, haunted by that familiar feeling that no matter what I did, I could never measure up to what I was supposed to be. But worse yet was the strange sensation—it seemed to be happening more and more—that I really wasn't much of a male.

Considering the nature of Dad's relationship with Mom— the way he disrespected her and was always criticizing her—I could only assume that what he really meant was something along the lines of "I hate you, too, John."

No matter what I accomplished or how hard I tried to impress him, Dad rarely praised me or made a fuss over me. Instead, his responses were tightly controlled and reserved. I never got an enthusiastic "I'm really proud of you!" or "You're the best son ever!" or "I'll always love you no matter what." This was especially hard for me because I was exactly the opposite of my dad—emotional, outgoing, highly verbal. The contrast between us reinforced just how different he and I were.

My mother's dominant personality got in the way of feeling much love there, either. With her, you didn't dare do anything to upset her or rock the boat. Even Todd, her husband, was afraid to confront her. I rebelled by deliberately provoking her. I'd point out that she wasn't treating us fairly. I'd play the game of pitting her against my father by talking badly about her when I was with him, and vice versa, reinforcing their negative feelings for each other. An added benefit was that I then gained favor with the parent to whom I was talking. Not until much later would I realize that I had only been hurting myself in the long run.

Meanwhile, I continued to feel alienated from other boys, confused about who I was, and wondering why I wasn't like them. I longed to fit in with them, but I knew I didn't.

Anne From the first day we met in my junior high school French class, I was attracted to Julie. She was somewhat masculine in appearance but had a delightfully feminine personality. Before long, I began to fantasize about her. To my great delight, she and I soon became great friends, and we spent many happy hours together, laughing, talking, and having fun.

It all looked perfectly normal to any observer, but my secret desires were taking an abnormal turn. As I became more and more convinced that Julie would be a wonderful life's partner, I started to imagine what it would be like to be married to her. Such a revolutionary thought caught me off guard. To make matters worse, I made the huge mistake one day of telling her, "I like you so much, Julie, that I want to marry you."

Not surprisingly, she instantly withdrew from our relationship. She didn't know what to do with me. I had been spending hours and hours at her house, but all at once I was no longer welcome. Feeling rejected and ashamed, I was still attracted to her, still wanted to be around her. There was no turning back, however. My words—and the desire behind them—had destroyed our friendship.

Meanwhile, some other friends and I began to experiment with alcohol. We managed to get our hands on a bottle of champagne at New Year's, and we enjoyed ourselves thoroughly.

Little by little, several of us entered into a negative, rebellious type of behavior. And that, not surprisingly, included smoking. I was all of 13.

My grandfather had died of lung cancer. My grandmother had emphysema, and it would eventually take her life. Needless to say, smoking was a sensitive subject in our family. And sure enough, my friend Marie and I got caught shortly after we started smoking when my mom smelled it on our clothes and confronted me.

"Mom," I asked, "didn't you ever want to do something that wasn't right?"

She looked at me as if I'd asked her the most ridiculous question in the world. "No," she said. "Of course not."

Every person on the planet has sinful desires, so she was obviously in major denial. But that conversation confirmed that I couldn't confide in my mother. I had all these imperfections, and she couldn't understand imperfections. If I couldn't go to her about smoking—when she couldn't relate to something as everyday as that—how could I talk to her about the real issues of my life—my attraction to girls and my confusion about boys?

During that same school year, I made friends with a boy who had a wild reputation. He was in what we called the "stoner" crowd, which meant he used drugs. And one day I asked him a very direct and important question: "Will you have sex with me this afternoon?"

And naturally, he said yes.

What would drive me to try to throw away my virginity? I couldn't have explained it. Was I trying to affirm that I really was a girl? Did I feel so unattractive that I wanted to gain some kind of acceptance? Or was my effort to have sex on my terms a way of remaining in control? One thing is certain: My self-concept was tragically distorted, and I felt terrible about myself.

The boy and I arranged to meet behind some building after school. Thankfully, he didn't show up at our rendezvous. I was disappointed and grateful at the same time. Later on that year, when he signed my yearbook, he used some really nasty terms to describe me. It was obvious that he and his friends thought I was trash. I had never felt worse about myself.

Meanwhile, my friend Marie's father discovered that she and I were smoking, and he responded in an interesting and wise way. "I want you two to sit out here on this porch," he instructed us, "and think of three good reasons why you should smoke."

We came up with three reasons quickly—to be cool, to act older, and something else I've since forgotten.

When he heard our list, he shook his head, dismissing our ideas with the wave of his hand. "No, no," he said with a laugh. "Those aren't good reasons. Sit out here and keep trying."

We sat there for a good hour and a half. We thought and talked and tried our best to come up with something.

Finally he came out to the porch again. "You couldn't come up with anything, could you?" he asked.

"No, nothing," I said.

He was going to tell my parents, but then he decided, "No, I'm not going to tell them, because you've obviously come to the conclusion that smoking isn't the right thing to do. So, since you're going to stop anyway, I'll keep all this to myself."

We smoked one more time after that. One day Marie and I went to a cigarette machine, but we weren't able to get our regular Marlboros. We tried something else, something entirely too strong for our taste. "This is gross!" I announced. "I'm done with this."

And, for me, that was the end of smoking. But it wasn't the end of my sexual confusion. If anything, that had only just begun.

John By the age of 14, I had an insatiable appetite for pornographic magazines, and I was getting good at making quick, thorough searches in my stepfather's closet. One time, I looked up on the shelf above his clothes and discovered a 35 mm movie projector.

This is interesting, I thought. *I haven't seen that up here before.*

A paper bag sat next to the projector, filled with dozens of small film reels. My parents were gone for the night and my sister was in bed asleep, so I got the projector down. I had run a similar projector at school, and I knew exactly what to do. I threaded a reel through the machine, turned on the light, and behold, a hard-core pornographic film materialized on the wall.

In all my life, I had never seen anything like those movies. They were heterosexual films, but I was absolutely mesmerized. From that day on, I watched those films whenever my parents were away. My craving for pornography became more and more intense.

Anne

Despite my parents' church attendance, I felt no sense of spiritual direction, and the thought of personal faith had never crossed my mind. But any talk about spirituality was interesting to me. My English class was taught by a student teacher who encouraged us to seek out our purpose in life by trying different spiritual paths. For the first time, I began to think about things like destiny and my long-term direction.

Another subject she introduced that also caught my attention was homosexuality. She told us about an author—I don't remember her name—who was a closeted lesbian. Her books were on the list of recommended reading, and I read a couple of them. I saw a lot of gender confusion in her work; she was a female author writing from a male perspective. *Do I fit here somewhere?* I asked myself. I found the idea of lesbianism exciting, though I still didn't identify myself as a lesbian.

During my sophomore year at Northgate High School, I joined the softball team. If ever I'd needed an excuse to be less feminine, this was a good one. All at once I was hanging around with a group of female jocks, some of whom were no more feminine than I was. And being part of their world helped counter my insecurities.

Eventually I got my braces taken off, which refined my appearance considerably and enhanced my social self-confidence. I also got contact lenses, which increased my coordination. I had always been good at sports, but the improvement was dramatic, and I began to excel. And I started to feel a little more comfortable with my tomboy persona.

John My mother and stepfather lived in the fast lane of society life. They threw wonderfully colorful parties, entertaining dozens of wild and eccentric friends, and alcohol was always available. I didn't think much about it until, sometime in the first two years of high school, I began drinking myself.

My friend Jim's father was an alcoholic. Jim and I would spend the night at each other's homes from time to time, like typical kids. His father made wine in their basement. Jim and I started drinking this home-brewed wine once his parents went to bed, and we would stay up drinking till two or three in the morning. His dad also had a fully stocked liquor cabinet.

One particular night after many weekends of this drinking-till-we're-drunk routine, Jim and I went downstairs to sleep in his large family room. Intoxicated out of our minds, we started experimenting sexually. We did this on several subsequent occasions as well, though it was a very different experience for each of us.

Whenever we played around that way, Jim would talk about wanting to have sex with girls. I would just listen to him, fixated on him. Girls never crossed my mind. I was far more interested in what the two of us were doing together.

Jim's mother was a nurse anesthetist, and she had access to all kinds of drugs. In their kitchen cabinet was a bottle of the liquid used to keep patients asleep during surgery. If you took the lid off, within 20 minutes the entire bottle would evaporate. Jim and I used to stick our noses up to the bottle, sniffing it and getting high.

One of those nights, after drinking and sniffing, Jim and I had our first real sexual encounter. I found it fascinating. This was the first time I'd had sex. It was two things at once—bizarre and enjoyable.

The next morning, a heavy blanket of shame descended over both of us. Jim was my best friend. We went to school together. We spent all kinds of time together. But we never talked about our experience. A silence between us engulfed what we had done and the taboo that surrounded it. Jim went on to be heterosexual, and it never happened again between us. We just continued as friends.

The next summer, three interesting things took place, each of them affecting me in a different way. One was that my father made a snide remark about gay men, and for the first time I thought he was directing his disapproval of homosexuality toward me.

Another was that my mother began to play the piano seriously, and as she played, I sometimes sang. I soon began to realize I had a good singing voice, especially on high notes. I auditioned for my high school's madrigal group and, to my surprise, was accepted. My musical "career" had begun.

The third event would eventually prove to be the most important of all. Clara, a classmate, called herself a "born-again Christian." With great persistence and patience, she had long tried to explain to me who Jesus is.

"You need to know Him, John," she'd say. "He's God's Son."

"But aren't we all God's children?" I'd counter. "I don't see what makes Jesus so different."

"Jesus is God's *only begotten Son,* John. Listen to this." Then she would squeeze her eyes tightly, concentrating hard so she could quote her favorite Bible verse by memory. "For God so loved the world that he gave his only begotten Son, that whosoever believes on him will not perish, but have everlasting life."

She wanted to make sure I understood that God had a "plan of salvation" for my life. Clara and I talked about Jesus for hours, and she encouraged me to pray and accept Him into my life, because some day He was going to return to the earth.

"I really want you to be ready, John," she explained, her face solemn with concern.

One night, sensing another impending fight between my mom and stepdad, I withdrew to my room. I sat there alone, and before long I was reflecting on Clara's message. My pulse began to speed up; I felt agitated and afraid. Was there really a place called heaven? Would I go there or wouldn't I? And what about hell? Apprehension chilled me—I was frightened by the possibilities.

"Jesus loves you, John," Clara had often told me. Now something quickened deep in my soul every time I thought about Him. Was it possible that Jesus really was God, and that He really might care about me?

By now I could hear angry voices arguing louder and louder in the next room. Our household was relentlessly chaotic, and I felt incredibly alone. Even sitting there and listening, I wondered if God could somehow fill the emptiness I felt.

Impulsively, I got up and opened my bedroom window. As a gentle breeze stirred the air around me and ruffled my hair, hope stirred in my spirit. I watched the moon gleaming silently, its light casting silver shadows on the trees and bushes outside. It felt as if, by opening my window, I had cleared a passageway to heaven.

All at once, my knees felt weak and my hands began to shake with some strange, new excitement. I knelt down beside the window. Lifting my eyes skyward, I quietly told God, "I know that I'm a sinner and that I won't go to heaven without You. Please forgive me and come into my heart."

The moment was breathtaking. My eyes flooded with tears of joy, and a warm sense of peace and expectancy rushed through me. The exhilaration continued long after my prayer was finished. I was so excited that I called my friend Jim and told him all about Jesus. My heart soared with joy all over again as he also prayed to receive the Lord into his heart and life.

As the following weeks passed, my fervor and enthusiasm carried on unabated. I started to attend a small Mennonite church in the area, and my faith flourished. I was even baptized—in a church elder's claw-foot bathtub.

Unfortunately, my parents weren't the least bit impressed with my newfound Christian faith. In fact, it began to scare them. After seeing me faithfully attend church for six months, my mother had had enough. She confiscated my Bible and demanded that I not read it. Soon I stopped attending church and going to the youth group. Within six months, I began to lose interest in God. I left Clara, Jim, and the whole Christian experience behind me. I didn't give it another thought for more than a decade.

Anne
⁓

"You know what, Anne? I pray for you every day." Leann, a young Christian, had befriended me, and when she said those words, for some reason I believed her. So when she persistently asked me to go to church with her, I finally agreed.

I hadn't really wanted to attend. But somewhere in my heart, I had a flicker of hope that God might be there. I longed to discover some aspect of the spirituality I'd heard about in my English class, and logically, church was where things like that were supposed to be found.

Sad to say, what I saw at Leann's church was even worse than the not-so-pleasant environment at high school. An assortment of unruly kids in the youth group were participating in a total party atmosphere. There was no alcohol and no one was using drugs, but you wouldn't have guessed it. Their actions were wild, and they talked to each other almost abusively. To my great disappointment, I felt even more insecure there than I did at school. *God's sure not here,* I told myself. *Maybe He's nowhere. In any case, I'm not coming back here again. Whatever the answer is, they don't have it.*

I flashed back to my first experience with God, which had taken place when I was in fifth grade. I'd been bored with one of the services at the Presbyterian church we were attending. My eyes had wandered upward, and as I looked at the ceiling, I saw a mysterious light. Where was it coming from? Somehow, it lit a spark of faith deep within me.

What is that? I asked myself. I looked around for the source but couldn't find it. *Wow, that's God!* I had concluded, convinced He was there.

As I returned home from the youth group, I recalled another incident that made me fairly sure God was somewhere. Right after I got my contact lenses, one of them popped out. A friend and I used a flashlight to look for it. We searched everywhere but couldn't find it. I was terrified that my mother wouldn't buy me a replacement.

Then I went into the bathroom to examine my clothes on the slim chance that it might have stuck to my shirt or gotten caught in my hair. Again, no luck.

All at once I got down on my knees and prayed, *God, please help me! I've got to find my contact.*

The next thing I did after giving up, praying, then giving up again, was to put my hand in my pocket. And there, lodged in the corner of my jeans pocket, was my contact. I was stunned! I stared at the contact in disbelief, and for a moment I felt like crying. Could it be that God had actually heard my prayer?

There was no other explanation—my contact had been found in an impossible location. It never could have gotten there on its own. It had to be God! From that time on, I knew He was somewhere. If He really was my "heavenly Father," as some people said, I wanted to find Him.

In the meantime, the situation with my earthly father wasn't getting any better at all.

I was excited about the prospect of learning to drive and

asked my dad several times if he would teach me. We lived a couple of blocks from the high school, and the blacktop parking lot was an ideal place to practice. Dad finally agreed to take me out in my sister's VW Bug so I could learn how to drive a stick shift.

Dad and I headed for the parking lot, where he had me practice how to start out in first gear. It sounded simple when Dad explained the process, but after 15 minutes of my trying hard to do just as he said, he became angry and frustrated.

"Why don't you just do what I'm telling you to do?" he said quietly, trying to restrain his annoyance.

"Dad, I'm trying. It's just that—"

"You kill the engine every single time," he interrupted, cutting off my explanation, "and if you'd just listen to what I'm telling you, it wouldn't happen!"

I was so humiliated. "Dad, I'm so sorry...." My voice broke. "I just can't seem to get it right."

I tried again. And again. I couldn't get the clutch to work right. My hands were shaking so much that I could hardly grip the gearshift knob, and I kept forgetting which way to push it.

Moments later, Dad left without another word. He simply got out of the car, slammed the door shut, and started walking to the house. Not only was I left alone with a vehicle that I couldn't drive, but far worse, I had once more been emotionally abandoned. How could I be such a failure? Why couldn't I ever get anything right?

John One time during my junior year in high school, I went into the boys' restroom to use the urinal. A guy named Travis came in a few seconds after me. Travis was known to be a homosexual, and he had a bad reputation. He walked up next to me, and before I knew what was happening, he reached over and grabbed me.

I was shocked and shaken. I could feel my heart pounding

in my throat, and my face began to sweat. I was frightened. I jerked back, turned away, and said, "No way! You're barking up the wrong tree! Get away from me!"

I zipped up and ran out of the restroom and down the hall. Trying to catch my breath, I thought about how disgusting his approach had made me feel. I didn't want to be part of anything Travis had in mind. Or did I?

Over the next days and weeks, I'd lie in bed at night or stand in the shower in the morning and wonder, *Why did he do that to me? Why did he feel he had the right to grab me like that?*

Sometimes I carried the thought a step further: *What if I'm just like him?*

Never before had I applied the term *gay* to myself, even though others had called me that for years. Despite their labels, I had never thought of myself that way. I had always wanted, in my mind, to get married someday.

I tried to think it all through carefully. Yes, I'd had crushes on girls, and when I held a girl's hand, it excited me. But at the same time, I couldn't look at girls sexually. I just saw them as friends. Instead, I constantly fantasized about sex with boys, even though—strange as it sounds—I didn't think I was gay.

Sometime during the next few weeks, my mother and Todd went out of town for the night. Vicky had gone to someone else's home. It was a Saturday evening, and at one point a knock came at the door. When I opened it, there stood Travis.

"Can I come in?" he asked.

Quickly overcoming my surprise and suddenly excited, I told him, "Sure." In he came, and before long we were both drunk. I was sitting on the floor, leaning against the couch and watching television. He was lying on the couch. This time I wasn't so shocked when he reached over and started stroking my chest. But, once again, feelings of revulsion came over me and I jerked away. All night, he kept teasing me like that, pleading with me to have sex with him.

"No, I'm not going to do that," I told him repeatedly. No

part of me really wanted him sexually. But by now I was enjoying the fact that somebody wanted *me* and was trying to pursue me.

A few days later, Mom and Todd filed for divorce. She and Vicky and I moved to a new apartment, and I settled in to being the "man of the house." My new role was short-lived, however.

In a matter of weeks, Mom took up with a guy that I believed to be just above a tramp. Her alcoholism had progressed to the point where she almost completely abdicated her role as a mother. She wouldn't go to the grocery store, barely paid the bills, and neglected to pick us up when she said she would, like getting my sister home from cheerleading practice. We got ourselves up and ready for school. When we had to find a new place to live, I contacted a Realtor and made the arrangements. Mom disappeared for days at a time and then came home drunk. Whereas the society pages had previously named her the best-dressed woman in the city, she now routinely went out in public without makeup and dressed in T-shirts and jeans. My sister and I didn't know what was going on.

Fortunately, she had inherited a trust fund from her father. Otherwise, we quickly would have been destitute, too.

During those troubled times, Vicky went to live with Dad in Portland, Oregon, where he had started a new restaurant business. Not long thereafter, Mom broke up with her boyfriend. By then she had become intolerable, raging and railing at me, miserable with herself. One night when she was very drunk, I became especially defensive. "I suppose you think every problem you've ever had is my fault!" I suggested bitterly.

"That's right!" she said thickly, fighting the alcohol and trying to form thoughts and words.

For me, it was nothing short of betrayal. I had been her emotional support for as long as I could remember, and for the past few months I had taken care of the household, too. How could she say such a thing? *If she doesn't love me,* I promised myself, *I'll find somebody who does.*

Anne In my senior year of high school, I managed to get myself involved with a somewhat more popular crowd. These kids drank and partied, and they usually invited me along. Jason was a handsome young man in this crowd. One night when we went out in somebody's van to drink, before I knew it, I was holding Jason's hand. By the next day, however, he didn't remember a thing about it. But from that night on, Jason became part of my fantasy life. In my mind, he was my boyfriend.

Cory was from a blue-collar family. He didn't have much money, and he lived in a rougher neighborhood. I lived in Walnut Creek, which was a white-collar area. Cory seemed to admire me simply because of my socioeconomic status. He would steal things from the store we worked at and give them to me as gifts. I didn't feel attracted to him, but even so, I thought that the attention he paid to me was kind of like dating.

Brian was my favorite, though. I had a crush on him and invited him to the senior ball. He went with me, and I managed to wear a soft green, spaghetti-strapped dress for the occasion. We went as friends and had a good time.

Attending the senior ball with Brian made me feel better about myself. Somehow, without even understanding my own behavior, I was trying to "fix" the sexual feelings I had for women and redirect them toward men. Unfortunately, I had a lot to learn about myself and homosexual attractions, and some of my lessons had to be learned the hard way.

After graduation, a group of us girls went to Hawaii together. By then, I had begun to look a little different—not quite as tomboyish as before. And during that time, I successfully concealed my feelings about girls, though it was very much in the back of my mind that what I wanted most of all was to go to a lesbian bar and meet the woman of my dreams.

Instead, our little group headed for the straight bars, which were full of sailors. I'm sure most of those seasoned girl watchers could immediately see that, despite our playfulness, we were really innocent. They must have quickly calculated that it would be no trouble to take advantage of us. And so we ended up with an assortment of navy men at our heels.

The result of our bar hopping was that I had sexual intercourse for the first time. Afterward, the young man, whose name was Mark, said, "Oh my gosh, you were a virgin!" And he actually began to weep.

Mark was African-American. He was good looking and very sensual. He appealed to me sexually, but not in a romantic or emotional way. I didn't feel I was in love with him or even had a crush on him. We were drawn together by sheer animal magnetism. I wish one of my friends had stopped me and said, "Are you sure you want to do this? Is this the right thing to do?" But nobody said a word.

I can still see myself sitting on the beach the day after our encounter, wearing a multicolored, two-piece swimsuit. While all my friends were laughing and kidding around, I was staring out at the ocean mournfully. A phrase repeated itself in my mind again and again: *I've lost something.* Regret welled up in my soul. I had handed over something priceless for no price at all. *Here, take it. Now it's gone.* I'd wanted to get rid of my virginity for years. Now it had finally happened, and I was filled with remorse.

Meanwhile, Mark actually took quite a liking to me. In fact, I think he fell in love with me. After I returned home, I struggled with my feelings—or, I should say, my lack of feelings—for him. I compared them to my feelings for women, and it was no contest. He couldn't reach my heart, and I wanted more than sexual pleasure. I wanted to be in love. I came to see that I could be physically attracted to a male, but I just couldn't surrender my heart to him. I couldn't fall for men the way they could fall for me.

With that issue in no way resolved, I entered my first year of college at the University of California at Santa Barbara. That's where I met Gina.

Looking
for Love

John

My pulse was pounding in my ears and my palms were sweaty before the three of us even got to the door. Once I stepped inside, I was nearly overwhelmed with excitement. For a couple of years, I had longed to visit a gay bar, drawn both by curiosity and by an ever-growing desire to meet a man who might be something like me. And now, to celebrate my 18th birthday, my friends Kevin (who had once confided to me that he was attracted to guys) and Jamie (a straight girl who was wild, crazy, and loved disco) had brought me to the "K."

And what a celebration it was!

The surroundings at the "K" were dazzling—disco lights, vivid colors, mirror balls. The air was heavy with the smells of alcohol, tobacco, marijuana, and men's fragrances. Once my eyes began to feast on the array of men who were there, I couldn't stop smiling.

Gay men of all ages, styles, and builds moved about like young animals, hoping to be admired and touched, wearing outfits that enhanced or revealed their most appealing physical qualities. They walked seductively and posed with intention, their eyes scanning all the other on-the-make males who crowded the place. The sound of music was deafening; the energy level was frenetic. Every man seemed to be looking for someone. Was anyone looking for me? I felt high and hopeful, and I hadn't even had a drink yet.

Once I had a little alcohol in my system, Kevin and Jamie were the last people I cared about hanging out with. I plunged into the scene, intoxicated by the powerful sexual energy in the room.

Until that night, I still hadn't really thought of myself as gay, though I knew my attraction to men was intense. Now I guessed that maybe Kevin and Jamie knew more about me than I knew about myself; perhaps that's why they'd brought me here. My physical response to the men at the "K"—men whose eyes disrobed me, whose hands caressed me, whose smiles warmly approved me—told me all I needed to know about what I really wanted.

By the end of the evening, I'd met at least one guy who very much attracted me. I didn't leave without having his name and address written on a cocktail napkin and stuffed in my pocket. Meanwhile, I had learned two things. First, being in a gay bar took my breath away, and I couldn't wait to go back. Second, I was finally convinced that I was a gay man. And I was ready, willing, and able to experience anything and everything the gay life had to offer.

Anne

Gina's hair was blonde and perfectly cut, and boys found her extremely attractive. She was wealthy, she knew how to wear makeup, and yet she somehow took a special interest in me. I wasn't sure why, but I was captivated by her attention.

Looking back, I think Gina saw me as a project. At the time, I had no sense of style. I still didn't know how to do my hair or dress well, and—as always—I was looking for a place to belong. I was the new girl on the block, and Gina took me under her wing. Sometimes she gave me the keys to her car. Other times, she let me hang around with her and get to know her boyfriends. It didn't take her long to dump one boyfriend and move on to the next gorgeous hunk waiting in line.

It didn't take me long to fall in love with Gina.

Gina wasn't lesbian at all, but she seemed to be afraid for people to get too close. Once she sensed any kind of emotional intimacy, she quickly pushed them away. I knew eventually that would affect me as well, because I was becoming increasingly attached and attracted to her.

One weekend, Gina invited me to her lovely home in Carmel, which meant we had to drive several hours together. I was ecstatic to be able to spend so much time with her. Gina was everything I wasn't—stylish, elegant, and trendy. On that trip she introduced me to my first espresso, took me shopping, and included me in her fashionable, up-scale world, even though I really didn't fit in. She never seemed to notice my lacks, and she was never ashamed to have me with her.

In Gina's view, she was my mentor. In my view, Gina was an unfulfilled sexual dream. And it was hopeless—there would never be a response from her, and I knew it.

During our visit to her home, her mother said, "Anne, you've got to look out for Gina. I don't want her to get in trouble with all those boys."

That's just what I wanted to hear. *Oh, I'll gladly take that role,* I silently vowed, because it was the role of a masculine protector. It fit perfectly into my childhood fantasy life. Even her mother seemed to know that Gina and I were destined to be together—without sex, of course.

John

As much as I loved hanging out at the "K"—and I spent more than my share of time hoping "he" would walk in—I didn't meet the man of my dreams there.

By now I was involved in Columbus, Ohio's, exclusive Fort Hayes Career Center for the Performing Arts, with hopes of a professional singing career. I had successfully auditioned and was performing as the male lead in Cole Porter's *Anything Goes.* During a resounding standing ovation one night, I caught the eye of a handsome man in the audience. His blue eyes met mine, and I was instantly captivated.

Later that night, I learned that his name was Ben and that he was gay. From the moment we met, we were more than a little attracted to each other.

Chills chased through me when Ben called the next day. I could tell from the sound of his voice that something wonderful was about to happen. "So, John, what do you like to do for fun?" he asked.

"Oh, I can think of a lot of ways to have fun," I responded with a laugh. "It depends on who I'm having fun with."

"Well, suppose you and I decided to have some fun together. What would you like to do?" Ben's voice was warm and playful.

"Why don't you give me some ideas?" I countered.

We were both enjoying ourselves thoroughly. Ben suggested, "Maybe I should come by your place and we could talk about it some more."

That's exactly what we did.

The better Ben and I got to know each other, the more we realized that we had experienced many of the same painful family dynamics. We spent hours talking, and Ben explained that he had dated girls in high school. He seemed pleased to report that young women were often drawn to him. This wasn't good news for me, because I already felt twinges of fear and jealousy at the thought of Ben being in love with someone else.

This was my first relationship, and I felt incredibly vulnerable. Before long, I started to keep close track of Ben's schedule, particularly regarding time he spent with other people. Although Ben managed to stay somewhat emotionally detached from me, I latched on to him for dear life. Morbid suspicion haunted me, and insecurity clouded our relationship, especially when men from Ben's past came and went out of his life.

Ben's response to my obsession was predictable—he began to pull away from me. And my response was also what you might expect—I hung on to him all the tighter.

I started to punctuate my time away from Ben with flirtations with other attractive men. Though I was emotionally glued to him, I was more than happy to enjoy the flattery of other men I met at the "K," especially when I thought it might make Ben jealous. At that point, I was sexually faithful to Ben, hoping for a monogamous, permanent relationship and naive about the games of gay life. But I was also learning to enjoy the pleasure of being admired, sought out, and pursued.

Anne

"Anne, do you want some 'shrooms?" Gina's current boyfriend was trying to introduce me to psychedelic drug use. I thought he meant mushrooms —the kind you eat—and I hated mushrooms.

"No, thank you!" I answered indignantly. "Are you kidding? I'm not touching those!"

I was so naive about drugs. I sometimes smoked a little pot with the drug users in the college dorm, but I never had the money to buy drugs for myself, and I'm not sure I would have done so anyway.

Gina, on the other hand, was deeply attached to the young man with the "'shrooms." He was suave and cool and had access to all sorts of things she shouldn't have been doing. My frustration with her behavior and my jealousy over her relationship with this latest boyfriend soon brought about the end of our relationship. I couldn't protect her, and I couldn't satisfy my feelings for her.

The more Gina was confronted with my jealousy, the more she withdrew from our friendship. Before long, she had become closer to a couple of other girls in the dorm, hanging out with them and ignoring me. My feelings for her were painfully strong, and I longed to be "in" with her again, her confidante, safe in that special place I'd had in her life. Instead, however, everything seemed to be slipping uncontrollably away from me.

I felt deeply hurt. I kept wondering what I had done wrong and if I could repair my mistakes. I tried desperately to talk to her. "Gina, I really miss hanging out with you," I pleaded. "Can't we just get together and talk like we used to? What have I done to make you avoid me?"

Gina stared at me with a completely detached expression. "I don't know what you're talking about, Anne," she insisted. "I'm not avoiding you. You're taking everything way too personally."

Eventually, Gina became impossible to approach, even for conversations. Her new female friends were always with her. I felt like one of her rejected lovers.

Gina had brought a special hope to me: She saw potential in me that no one else had seemed to see, she had entrusted me with her secrets, and she had believed in me in ways that made me dream of a new, exciting life. She had captured a large part of my heart, and now I was brushed aside without explanation.

As a last-ditch effort, I knocked on her dorm room one day. "Here are your car keys, Gina," I began, tears coursing down my face. "I realize our relationship is over, so I won't be needing them anymore."

Gina simply took them from my hand without offering any words of confirmation or denial. Without so much as a shrug of her shoulders, she went back into her room and resumed a conversation with her friends. Rejected and humiliated, I rushed outside and tried to find a solitary place to cry. I felt so alone, so abandoned, and worse than ever about myself. Yet, in the days that followed, Gina didn't even seem to notice.

I was convinced by now that I was lesbian, and as far as I was concerned there would be no more faking it. But just to make sure, I made one final reality check. I invited Mark, the boy I'd been with in Hawaii, to the dorm. At the time, he was stationed somewhere in Washington.

"Mark," I explained, "I really want to see you."

I did want to see him, but not for the reasons he imagined.

Mark went to the expense of flying himself to Santa Barbara. Once we were together, I tested my feelings toward him. Essentially, I didn't have any. I discovered that I could have sex with him, but I was unable to make any emotional connection with him at all.

Meanwhile, Mark had really fallen for me. He tried to share his life with me, showing me pictures of his home and family, even hinting about our getting married. But I was interested only in using him as a sort of a sexual litmus test. To make matters worse, in an ill-conceived effort to be "honest," I told him all about my dream to be with a woman. He was absolutely shattered, and I never heard from him again. To this day, I regret the way I treated him. I devastated him. I used him as a pawn. And, until years later, I didn't even realize what I had done.

John I enrolled at Ohio State University the fall after my high-school graduation, and Ben and I moved into the dorm together. My expectations were, to say the least, unmet. We found it impossible to maintain a sexual relationship in a room shared with two very straight, very observant young men. Our bunk beds weren't especially conducive to romantic trysts, either, and we tried desperately to hide our gayness from our roommates, which further cramped our style.

Over the long Thanksgiving weekend, we went our separate ways to be with our families. While at home, I received a call from Brandi, a meddlesome female friend. "John," she began with a wicked giggle, "you'll never guess who I saw Ben with last night."

My heart sank. "Really? Who?" I asked, afraid of what I was about to hear.

Brandi told me that Ben had been hanging out with one of his ex-boyfriends. I was already missing him terribly. Now I was devastated.

When I returned to school, I confronted Ben angrily. He denied everything, but I refused to believe him and continued to harangue him unmercifully. Hours of argument dragged by, each of us unwilling to give an inch. I believed with all my heart that Ben had been unfaithful. He stubbornly disagreed. The most I could get out of him was a lame apology for "whatever I've done to offend you." The matter was left unresolved. The relationship was permanently damaged.

We continued to visit the "K" together, but our drinking increased and our fights—public and private—intensified. By the time Christmas had come and gone, Ben had admitted that he had, indeed, been with someone else. Worse yet, he let me know in no uncertain terms that he was through with me as a roommate. "Your constant attacks are making me sick," he announced one day, his voice tinged with bitterness. He was, in fact, troubled by an ulcer, and I probably wasn't helping to improve his condition.

I tried everything in my power to keep Ben in my life. I begged, I pleaded, I asked his forgiveness, I promised him anything and everything I might have to offer. But it was all to no avail. It became apparent that he didn't love me with the kind of unconditional love I'd always dreamed about, a love I'd imagined a gay lover would offer me.

My heart was broken, and I couldn't control my tears. How could I live without Ben? I was sure I couldn't continue in college without him, so I dropped out of Ohio State. I had never felt so alone.

Anne

After losing Gina, I was sick at heart, unable to deal with the loss. The loneliness was killing me; the pain was so intense that, for the first time in my life, I decided to seek professional help. I called around campus until I found a gay peer counselor. I wanted to talk to a man, hoping to avoid a situation where I could become too emotionally involved with another woman. I was confused enough.

My counselor was a gay Catholic. Although I had little understanding of the Christian faith, I'd heard enough to know that most Christians believe homosexuality is wrong, and the idea of being on the wrong side of God nagged at me.

"Look," I explained, "I'm really having this trouble with my lesbian feelings. I'm really not what you'd call a Christian, but I keep having these regrets about wanting to follow my feelings into homosexuality. I've read passages in the Bible like Genesis 19 about Sodom and Gomorrah and Leviticus 18:22, and I just don't know what to do."

The man smiled kindly at me, nodding his head in understanding. "Well, the most important thing for you to understand is that you can be a Christian and still be gay," he said. "The Bible isn't really against homosexuality. After all, God is love, and the Bible never speaks against love of any kind. Those verses you mentioned are in the *Old* Testament. Jesus said to love your neighbor, and that's what homosexual attractions really are—love."

As much as I wanted to believe him, I couldn't accept his interpretation of the Scripture passages. On the other hand, I felt no obligation to obey the Bible. I remembered the empty, hopeless experiences I'd had with church and youth groups. Church had never offered even a glimpse of the hope and new life that Gina had temporarily provided, and she wasn't even homosexual! I imagined the fulfillment I could have with another woman who would love me in return.

Besides, was God really there anyway? He seemed like a vague, distant concept, nothing but an illusion blocking my way to happiness with a lifetime woman lover. Evolution—the idea that all life had developed without a Creator-God—seemed to offer a far more reasonable explanation of the world and my sadness than did the Bible. It also provided an excuse to dismiss the Bible and its God as obsolete and unrealistic.

It really wasn't a difficult decision.

I decided to whisk everything under a rug and simply say, "God doesn't exist." I concluded that I had to throw Him completely away in order to pursue what I wanted. No matter what my counselor said, I knew I could never find fulfillment as a lesbian if I tried to fit my lesbianism into a world where God was in charge.

My counselor did manage to get me involved in a lesbian support group offered by our campus's active gay and lesbian alliance. I started attending gay meetings and events. And it was at one of those events when a deep, piercing realization wrenched my soul. I was listening to this panel of parents who said, "My kids have told me about their homosexuality and lesbianism, and I have accepted them. I love their idea of love, and I don't see any problem with it. I've gotten over my homophobia."

That sounded good to me, and when the meeting ended I wanted to thank one of the mothers who had just proclaimed her love and acceptance for her son and her son's lover. At that time, I wasn't especially intimidating in my appearance. Although I was dressing in a unisex style and had a boyish haircut, I wasn't wearing leather or spikes or anything like that. Yet as I approached this woman to talk to her, she looked up at me, and a look of repulsion and recoil immediately froze her face.

Her expression said it all. No matter what declaration she'd made to the group minutes before, her silent, inward response was, "This is *not* okay. I don't feel comfortable with this, even though I'm trying to tell everybody that I do. I'm terrified and horrified by people who are consumed by homosexuality and lesbianism."

The woman shrank into a group of 10 other parents, quickly and intentionally eluding me. I walked away. And I walked away thinking that even though all those people were trying to prove that everything was just fine between them and their kids, it wasn't fine at all. The message I heard was loud and clear: *No matter how much we deny it, there's something wrong with homosexuality. It's not supposed to be this way.*

I rushed blindly out into the night and headed for the library, where I was fairly sure I would be alone. I cried all the way there, tears streaming down my face. I was so distraught that I could hardly find my way. I sobbed for a good half hour, sitting all alone in a little library cubicle. It was Friday night, and no one else was there. Everyone was having a good time partying—everyone except me.

For some reason, I suddenly found myself praying. I said, *God, if You're out there, I want to know who the real God is, and I don't want any interference from any other spiritual force that claims to be You. I don't know if You're a Hindu god or what You are, but I want to know You. Will the real God please stand up?*

I paused, wiped my face off, and, faced with a sudden and terrible thought, I continued, *Oh, please don't be the Christian God, because I really want to pursue homosexuality. But if You are the Christian God, then this is what I need...*

I made up a laundry list of needs right there on the spot: *God, I need to meet someone who is leaving or has left the gay life herself. Someone who is a Christian and is working through these things and is real honest with the contradictions she sees. I need this person to have short, brown hair, to be attractive to me, to play Frisbee with me, to ride a bike—to ride a bike double...*

There I was, praying to the God that I had recently decided didn't even exist and that I was still *hoping* didn't exist, saying, *Look, if this is You, here's what You'll have to do to convince me that You're real. Here's how You can prove to me that You're interested.*

I had no knowledge of spiritual warfare, no understanding that there's an active evil force called Satan in the universe, seeking to destroy us (see, e.g., 1 Peter 5:8). But I knew I didn't want some impostor sticking his nose into my business. So I prayed without having any knowledge, and I prayed the right prayer. I cried out, from the deepest core of my being, for what I had thought only lesbianism could give me:

God, I just want to be loved. I just want to be unconditionally loved.

John

After Ben left, my world began to change. I met new people, started going to new clubs, and finally started to enjoy life again. I met a woman named Amy who was a singer. Though she was not homosexual, she enjoyed showing me new elements of the Columbus gay social scene.

I had physical relationships with several men along the way, but none of them seemed to be especially satisfying. Having had a relationship that was both sexual and emotional, I now struggled with the emptiness of one-night stands. Still, the number of encounters increased, and my need for sexual activity seemed to be intensifying.

One day during a particularly lonely week, I found myself longing for a real "relationship," for something more meaningful than the kinds of encounters I was experiencing. Impulsively, I called Ben just to talk. I started the conversation by asking him to forgive me for my past possessiveness.

He was more receptive than I had dared hope, and he agreed to come over to my apartment that evening. We talked for a while, had a few drinks, and ended up in bed together. As much as Ben and I enjoyed each other's company, I was disappointed that things weren't the same as they had once been. Still, I liked Ben a lot and hoped we could manage to remain friends.

Meanwhile, my quest continued. One night, after an unsatisfying episode with a man I'd met, I started wondering if I was being unrealistic, hoping to find meaning in a relationship with another man. Maybe I couldn't have it all. Maybe I should just live it up, enjoy every bit of sex I could get, and forget the idea of a "steady" relationship. Lots of men obviously wanted me, but I'd always held back, hoping to find "Mr. Right." Why wait any longer for someone who probably didn't exist?

Anne I began to have dreams about Jesus—three altogether—out of the blue. Soon after the third one, I was sitting with some of my Jewish friends at the dining commons, and one of them made a really nasty wisecrack about Jesus. Deep anger welled up within me as soon as I heard her remark.

"I don't make fun of your religion," I burst out, "so why are you doing this to Jesus?"

"What are you so uptight about?" she countered with a frown. "What's your problem, anyway?"

I had shocked her with my vehemence. I had also shocked myself. I didn't have a relationship with Jesus. I didn't think He was especially significant. I didn't even know who He was. But now, after those dreams, I began to ask, *Who is Jesus? Who does He say He is?*

It was March 1982, and I kept running into a woman named Lynn. One day I watched her talking to a punk rocker with the utmost gentleness, kindness, and respect. The weird-looking girl had a ridge of bright pink hair sticking straight up into the air, and nobody else would have given her the time of day. But there was Lynn, sharing her class notes with her, telling a messed-up kid whatever she needed to know. I was impressed.

One of the times I ran into Lynn was at a softball game, where I had felt a strong attraction to her, thinking perhaps she was a lesbian, too. But when I asked a friend of hers about her, I learned that Lynn was a Christian. Soon I was so attracted to her that when I leaned forward to introduce myself in class one day, I was shaky and could hardly talk. I managed to get the words out the second try.

"Didn't I meet you at the softball game?" I whispered.

We struck up a friendship on that day. Then all the things I'd asked God to do began to happen, one after another: One Saturday Lynn played Frisbee with me; another day, she talked me into riding double on a bike. She even had short, brown hair. But I had forgotten all about my prayer, too distracted by my infatuation with Lynn to remember what I had prayed.

Lynn seemed to like having me around. We went for walks on the beach, and for me it was so romantic. She admitted that she'd had lesbian desires before, too, and she responded a little to my advances. Before long, my feelings became overpowering. We were sharing a wonderful moment one day, sitting on the beach together, and I said, "You know, if I could, I would marry you. I think I'm in love with you."

Lynn paused and looked deeply into my eyes. I saw a deep compassion and tenderness there and not a trace of rejection. But she didn't miss a beat. "You know," she responded, "I'm really married to Jesus. I do care for you as a friend, Anne, but my heart has to be committed to Christ."

With that, she set up a boundary with me, making it clear that we would not enter into a sexual relationship.

In the midst of my disappointment, I also felt a little relieved that I wasn't losing our relationship. Lynn possessed a type of character that I hadn't encountered before. I believed every word she said, and even though I still longed for fulfillment of my feelings, I didn't feel rejected. I didn't understand Lynn's tenderness, but I kept the memory of it close to my heart.

Again and again I noticed that something other-worldly seemed to light up Lynn's face and attitude. I also sensed a joy in her that I associated with purity. She became much more transparent with me about wanting to please Jesus in all areas of her life. At work she was diligent, not looking for the easy way out or making excuses. In her studies, she was dedicated and helped me to learn better study techniques. She worked hard to complete her assignments and was there to help when I or others didn't understand something. And none of this was done pridefully. I adored Lynn for all these things and more.

On the other hand, Lynn's ambivalence confused me. She allowed me to embrace her, and we would study lying on the bed together. I was always craving more, but she retained just enough reserve not to let anything happen. Still, she brought me roses occasionally, and she wrote affectionate little notes, seeming to play a romantic game of cat and mouse.

Even so, I saw something greater than romance in Lynn; I saw Jesus. Sometimes in her eyes, in her face, I saw the reflection of something so much higher. And that continued to draw me further toward God, even though our relationship wasn't perfect.

In the midst of all this romantic excitement, I still grappled with the dreams about Jesus that I'd had before meeting Lynn. One day at lunch I asked my Catholic friends Beth and Gail, "What is Jesus? Is He God?" assuming they'd have a clearer understanding than the Jewish women had. "Explain to me who He is."

Beth answered, a bit robotically, "Jesus is the Christ, born of Mary, a good man, a prophet ... you know."

"But what did He say about Himself?" I persisted.

After a long pause, Beth glanced at Gail and shrugged. "I don't know what to tell you, Anne," she replied. "I only know what I've been told."

Neither Gail nor Beth could give me a satisfactory answer. None of my friends could. Though they had been through catechism and other church traditions, they didn't seem to know Him at all.

Later that day, as Lynn and I were walking across campus together, we saw a table for a Christian organization called Campus Ambassadors, directed by a Jewish man who had become a Christian. Because I had so many Jewish friends, I felt comfortable talking with him. "Look," I said, "I'm just trying to figure out who Jesus said He was. None of my friends can answer these questions. Do you have anything to offer, some material that I can read?"

"No, but we have this class called Evangelism Training that goes through all these things," he answered. "Do you want to attend?"

I signed up and attended for a month, and there I began to find my answers. I especially took notice as Matthew 16 was read from the Bible. In that chapter Jesus asked Peter, "Who do you say I am?" Peter answered, "You are the Christ, the Son of the living God" (verses 15-16).

One of the meetings focused on the question "Why is there

evil in the world?" That's where I first learned that there's a spiritual realm and an evil being named Satan who is bent on our destruction. It seemed to explain a great deal about current events: serial murders, rapes, and other brutalities that people were committing all around the world.

As all my own thoughts and explanations of evil started to fall flat, I asked every question I could think of. "Isn't evil the result of poor education?" I suggested. "Or maybe it's caused by mental retardation?"

But someone always had a sensible answer. For instance, one person responded, "How can you say ignorance is the problem when the German population under Hitler was very well educated?"

Finally I asked the director, "Doesn't the idea of a personal devil seem a little old-fashioned to you?"

"Just because it's an old idea doesn't mean it's a wrong one," he replied.

On and on we went, and in that setting, I experienced a new kind of intellectual freedom and heard questions and answers that I'd never even thought about before. Things became clearer to me about how the universe runs and why. Something great and powerful was at work, not only in the universe, but also in my life.

As days turned into weeks, I was beginning to wonder what my response to that Something should be.

John I returned to Ohio State at the beginning of the next spring quarter, in 1982, but by summer I had lost my job, and I reluctantly began looking for another. I asked around and watched for signs in windows. When time passed and I was still unemployed, I started my search in earnest by looking through the classified section of the *Columbus Dispatch*. Nothing sounded especially interesting at first. Then I noticed a two-word heading: "Escort Services."

My imagination surged with excitement. Immediately I flashed back to some of the porn stories I'd read and seen in films. One particular plot centered on a handsome, gay prostitute in New York who was rich, sexy, and glamorous. I envisioned myself in a similar role, meeting fascinating men and living in a fabulous home. I read the ad twice, the second time more carefully. "Our clients deserve the very best," it said. "Male and female escorts wanted."

I couldn't help but smile. It might be the best of both worlds, I decided, blurring the edges between my personal life and my work. Besides, what did I have to lose? I called and set up an appointment.

To my amazement, I was just the kind of male escort they were looking for to provide companionship for their "special male clients." The man who interviewed me was straight and a little tacky looking, but I chose to ignore his appearance. He explained that he offered his clients nude conversation, nude massage, and nude modeling.

"Are you sure I won't get arrested ... or something?" I asked lamely.

He smiled condescendingly and quickly assured me that everything was legal and risk free. I mistrusted him implicitly, but I needed a job, so I accepted his offer.

I wasn't particularly concerned about my job description. My family had no way of finding out what I was doing. Dad had relocated in Portland, Oregon, and by now he and I barely spoke. As for my mother, I simply informed her that I was working for a private investigating service.

So it was, with hardly a second thought, that I began my career as a male prostitute.

Anne

Whenever I would pray at the Campus Ambassadors meetings, I made an effort to sound just like all the other students. I wanted so much to fit in with the group. But one night as we bowed our heads, I felt a Presence that seemed to permeate the room. An incredible Being—the Holy Spirit—had enveloped us in gentleness, kindness, authority, reliability, and credibility.

But I also sensed I was on the outside looking in. I knew there was something I wanted among all these people. They had it and I didn't. I could almost reach out and touch it, as if it were a soft, cushioning wall around me. It was that real. I thought, *They have what I want. I know that's what I want. And I couldn't care less about anything else in my life. I want that more than anything, including homosexuality.*

Any desire I had toward a woman was nothing compared to what I recognized there. Afterward, I talked to the pastor. He was great. He asked, "So what's holding you back?"

"Look," I told him, "I'm gay, but I want this Presence. I want what you guys have. I know I do."

He nodded his head thoughtfully and replied, "Well, that's a bit of a conflict." He explained it all to me biblically, from passages like 1 Corinthians 6:9-10, and concluded, "Anne, there's nothing to prevent you from accepting God's grace. It's just that you can't continue to have it have both ways. You are either going to surrender your life to Christ or you're not."

I nodded and said, "I understand."

"If you decide to surrender your life to Christ," he continued, "and if you pray the prayer I told you about, believe me, Satan will want you back, and he will fight for you. He doesn't want you to enter God's kingdom." Briefly, he explained the concept of spiritual warfare to me, and he read in Ephesians 6 that God gave Christians armor and some weapons to use against Satan. The pastor finished with a generous offer: "If you decide to pray and ask Jesus into your life, you can call me day or night at this number." He scribbled his phone number on a piece of paper. "Let me know and I'll pray for you. I'll ask God to protect and guide you."

I went home feeling nervous beyond belief because I knew

exactly what I was going to do. After only a few minutes of hesitation, I knelt down by my bed and prayed, *God, I'm a sinner. Please forgive my sins. I accept You as my Lord, and I want You to run my life. I want to be plugged into Your power and Your guidance, and I want to live according to Your plan in the Bible.*

Two seconds later, the phone rang. It was my friend Sarah, a Jewish lesbian who had recently introduced me to the lesbian scene in Santa Barbara through gay movies, lesbian bars, and the women's rugby team at UCSB. Her voice vibrant with excitement, she said, "Anne, come over! I really need to talk to you right now."

It was 10 o'clock on a Wednesday night. Wednesday night was not party night. What was going on?

"Sarah, I'll be right over," I said. I put the phone down and laughed hilariously. I felt like shouting, "This is perfect! It really happened. I'm a Christian! I'm a Christian! God's in my life!" What the pastor had said had happened, just as he'd said. And Satan's best effort to get me back had only served to reinforce in me what God had just done.

All at once, an incredible joy bubbled up out of me from nowhere. I was forgiven! I was part of God's family! I had purpose in my life! God's Spirit overwhelmed me right then and there.

When I arrived at Sarah's house, my face was absolutely radiant. Someone took pictures of us that night, and when I looked at those photographs later, I could see that my eyes were sparkling. The outward part of me hadn't changed yet; I was still as athletic-looking as before. But my eyes revealed the new, unexplainable thing that was going on inside. There was life within me where nothing had been before.

I told Sarah everything that had happened. She looked at me with some confusion and asked, "Anne, are you sure you're doing the right thing?" She didn't talk to me for a long time after that.

Ironically, in the days and weeks that followed, the main

temptation came from my friend Lynn. Although she still maintained that she was married to Christ, her feelings for me seemed to change. Now I had something more to offer. With Christ's new life within me, I was more attractive. I sensed that she was becoming sexually interested in me.

The two of us got baptized together at Calvary Chapel, Santa Barbara. Lynn was a born-again Christian, but she had never been baptized. I felt like a new woman coming out of the water. I wore a red shirt signifying my former dirtiness. And as I came out of that water, I really felt like a brand-new creature. In my spirit, I knew I was clothed in white even though I was wearing a red shirt. And I remember having not one impure thought toward Lynn for a long time after that. I could treat her like a sister and sense absolutely no inappropriate attraction.

John My job at the escort service continued, and, predictably, it involved far more than nude modeling or conversation. At first it was difficult for me to "perform" sexually for stranger after stranger. Before long, I was wrestling with a whole new set of negative emotions. Day after day, time and again, I felt used and discarded. Prostitution is a lonely business.

The few friends who knew what I was doing were concerned, warning me about vice cops, rape, or even murder. I tried to shake off their words, but even though I was making a huge amount of money, fears nagged at me.

Meanwhile, my loneliness intensified dramatically. No matter how many times I had sex each week, I still longed in my heart for love and acceptance. Ben had been living with another man, but rumor was that their relationship was on the rocks. Needing someone to talk with, one night I asked him to drop by my apartment.

Ben and I didn't have sex that night. As we talked, I found myself pouring out my heart to him. "My life is a mess!" I admitted. "Even though I live well—a nice apartment, lots of money—there's this awful pain inside me."

"Have you ever thought about seeing a counselor?" he asked.

"You mean a therapist?"

"Exactly. I know you're strong, and you can make it through alone. But wouldn't it be helpful to talk to someone with a different point of view? Someone who understands people?"

"To tell you the truth, Ben, I've never thought about it."

"Why don't you call the Gay Alliance at the school? Maybe they can refer you to somebody."

That conversation led me into the office of a clinical psychologist, Dr. Brian Taylor, who is gay himself and a highly regarded specialist in issues facing homosexual men.

In our first session, I told Brian a great deal about my family background, about the emptiness I felt, and about my troubled relationships with Ben and others. I told him about my drinking and the anonymous sex I had experienced. But I didn't have the courage to tell Brian about my job and the filthiness I felt whenever I thought about it.

Anne

After I trusted in Jesus, some women associated with Campus Ambassadors taught me more about the Bible and prayer. I was very open with them and with all the people at Campus Ambassadors about my struggle with lesbianism. In fact, I stood up in a large-group meeting and told them all exactly what had happened to me. Everybody knew, and I wasn't shy about it. I wasn't rejected, either.

But they really didn't know what to do with me. They didn't know how to encourage me to grow except by reminding me to study the Bible, pray, and continue having good social times with other Christians. They could offer no specific help when it came to my personal life.

For example, my memory of being molested at the age of four had remained buried until one point during my relationship with Gina. When it came back, it brought with it an enormous amount of shame. Now, when I told the pastor of that campus group about it, he thought for a minute and then responded carefully, "You know what? I want you to go see a counselor in downtown Santa Barbara. He's affiliated with a good church, and I'd like you to talk to him, because I'm really not good at counseling."

So I went to see the counselor. "I'm struggling with lesbian feelings; that's why I'm here," I told him on my first visit. "I want to resolve them. I want to know what's going on." I then explained that I had been sexually violated when I was younger. "Now, all of a sudden, I'm feeling incredible shame and anger about it," I said.

"Really?" he responded. "You know, that could be a key to why you have these lesbian feelings."

I didn't understand how there could be any connection whatsoever. But this counselor made an interesting suggestion. He asked me to try to see the teenage boy who molested me as being responsible. That was a whole new thought for me. I had never considered saying, "Look, it was your responsibility. You were 14, and I was just four. I didn't know any better, but you did."

The counselor explained that the older boy would have been responsible even if I had made the advances. He should have said, "No, that's not right. We can't do this." That would have been the appropriate response, and he had every opportunity to respond like that. But he chose not to. Under no circumstances could it have been my fault.

Later, the counselor asked me to write a letter to the boy expressing how much the episode had hurt me. He didn't want me to send it but simply to confront him as a molester. I did everything the counselor suggested, and as I began to express some of my feelings, my sense of shame diminished.

But the more I reflected on these things, the more I became aware of my anger. *How could you do that to me?* I thought repeatedly. *I was just a little girl! I was so innocent and naive. How could you take advantage of my curiosity for your own purposes?*

My rage was as intense as if I had been raped, and I struggled with it for a year. I began to identify with that little girl, wanting to protect her, angry with the young man. And as that little girl became me, I could see how deeply I had been affected by the boy's actions, how hurt and scared and alone I had felt.

"I'm beginning to feel things that I've put aside for years," I told my counselor at that point, feeling alarmed by the intensity of my feelings. "I must have banished them to some hidden, shame-filled place in my memory."

"As an adult," he asked, "can you see that that incident never should have happened? That you were robbed of your innocence and sense of value as a little girl? I think the anger you're feeling is the anger an adult would feel about a daughter who has been robbed of her innocence."

"Except the little girl was *me*. You know," I told him, shaking with emotion, "getting in touch with my loss is almost overpowering to me, my anger is so intense."

After several sessions with my counselor, I no longer made excuses for the boy's behavior. But I didn't take the blame myself, either, as if the incident had been my fault. I recognized and felt how betrayed I had been.

"I'm just so full of anger at the boy himself," I said. "I'm having a hard time seeing him as just another fallen person. I see him as evil, as someone who robbed me and didn't even know or care what he had taken."

I didn't know how to forgive, but from my Bible reading, I knew I needed to. Yet somehow I couldn't do it. Wisely, the counselor didn't try to force the issue. Instead, he suggested that I grieve. He also asked me to write down my own sins and then burn the paper as a demonstration that I'd been forgiven. That was very helpful. But even after all this, I still didn't see any connection between the molestation and my lesbianism.

Samantha Parker-Davis was another counselor whom I saw the following summer. At the beginning of our series of sessions, she asked me to describe my relationship with my family. It must have seemed like pulling teeth for her.

"So Anne, what's your relationship like with your mother and father?" she began.

I stared at her with a bewildered expression on my face. "I … I don't know."

"What do you mean?"

I paused, trying to find the words I needed. "I mean I don't know how to explain my family to you."

Fortunately, Samantha persevered, and in later sessions she started to touch on some deeper issues. She asked me to talk to her as if she were the various people involved in my sexual molestation. "Anne," she asked, "what would you say to me about what happened if I were your mother?"

I thought and struggled for a while. Finally I said, "Mom, where were you when this happened? Why couldn't you tell something was wrong and ask me questions until you figured it out? I didn't feel like I was nurtured or cared for, and I felt so vulnerable. My whole secure world was crashing down, and you didn't step in and figure it out."

Samantha nodded her head and continued. "Now suppose I'm the teenage boy who took advantage of you. What would you say to me?"

That answer came more easily. "I'd say: How could you take advantage of me? I'm angry and feel used. You should have known better. Why did you have to have all that pornography? I got entangled in your sin, and it warped me. Sex and sensuality became the big, confusing focus of my life."

Samantha listened closely and made a few notes as I spoke. "Okay, Anne. Now I'm your father. What would you like to say to me?"

I sighed deeply and shook my head. "Dad," I began, "I could never think of you as my protector. You were so absent in my life, traveling so much for your work. And when you were home, you were emotionally absent. I don't think you even noticed the way I was changing. Why weren't you paying attention? Couldn't you see that I needed your attention and affection to prove to me that males are worthy of trust? It seemed like you had no idea what was going on in your children's hearts, and you just expected everything to turn out well on its own. You weren't available emotionally to me."

Samantha then asked me a question I'd never really thought about before: "What about God, Anne? What would you like to say to Him?"

I looked at her uncertainly. "Is that … a good idea?" I asked.

She smiled and affirmed, "Go ahead, Anne."

I took a moment to think through what I wanted to say. Finally I spoke. "God, I felt so hurt and misunderstood and angry when that boy exposed himself to me. I was a devastated, lonely little girl without direction and getting more messed up by the day. How could You let that happen to me? Why didn't You stop that boy from experimenting with me sexually and turning my world upside down? Didn't You care enough to prevent him from taking advantage of me?"

After the counseling session, I went outside and found an isolated corner of the building where I could further express my feelings to God. As I wept, curled up and hugging my legs, I felt free to just hurt in His company. I didn't expect any quick answers, nor did I feel relief from the pain. I simply sobbed for that lonely little girl, crying out to be protected and understood. Crying out to be held in safety and reassured of her daddy's love. Crying because of the lack of provision for her emotional needs in her family.

As the minutes ticked by, I embraced that four-year-old child, crying out to her heavenly Father on her behalf. *How could my life have been so marred, the value of my life so tossed aside, when You really do exist?* I asked Him angrily.

Seemingly out of nowhere, a verse came to mind that I really didn't want to think about: "Praise be to the God and Father of our Lord Jesus Christ, the Father of compassion and the God of all comfort, who comforts us in all our troubles, so that we can comfort those in any trouble with the comfort we ourselves have received from God" (2 Corinthians 1:3-4).

That didn't help me at all. It seemed like such a pat answer during so much pain.

Even more painfully, I started to think about the concept of mankind's free will. I knew that God allows people to do wrong things that hurt others. I was also aware that God does not want puppets but disciples, worshipers in spirit and in truth. The consequence of this freedom is that some people will not submit to His ways and therefore do evil.

When I spoke to Samantha again, I told her what had happened. "I was pouring my heart out to God, and by the time I'd finished, I was beginning to understand what happened," I concluded.

She nodded, smiling a little sadly. "It doesn't lessen the pain, but at least it gives you a sense of God's presence," she observed. "Didn't you feel as if His Spirit was speaking to you?"

"I did, even though I wasn't sure I wanted to hear what He had to say."

At group therapy sessions that Samantha invited me to attend, women described their lives and their current struggles. Several women had been sexually molested. I began to see that their emotional damage from those events was not unlike my own, even though they were heterosexual. In fact, many had been through much worse and were dealing with abusive situations even now. This made a deep impression on me.

In our last session at the end of the summer, Samantha helped me with career guidance, and I decided to do something I enjoyed more than accounting. I changed my major to physical education—a typical lesbian thing to do—and that meant transferring to a different school to pursue my degree. I applied to Cal State Hayward and was accepted for my senior year.

At the beginning of that year, I met an interesting young master's student. She was bright. She had a lot of attractive qualities. She was a devout Christian.

Her name was Mary.

John

My departure from prostitution wasn't well planned. In fact, it would be more accurate to say that I just escaped with my life. During a scary encounter with a strange "customer," I fled in the nick of time. I never went back to the escort service.

After I left, however, I kept up a friendship with Racine, a woman who had worked with me there. She'd earned her living acting out several variations of the same job description, none of them respectable. Racine had been a Mafia mistress and a New York hooker, and now she was trying to stay alive as an escort in Columbus, Ohio. Time was passing, and things weren't exactly looking up for her.

One day not long after I quit, Racine called me. "I've got a great idea!" she gushed. "You've gotta come over right now!"

When I got to her home, she was bursting with excitement. "John, why should we work for someone else?" she asked. "Let's start our own escort service!"

"Racine, give me a break!" I responded.

"No, wait! Hear me out," she urged. "I've done this before, and it's really no big deal. You and I will work the phones, and we won't have to turn tricks unless we want to." She took a big drag on her cigarette and exhaled loudly. "So what do you think?"

The more I thought about it, the more it started to sound like a reasonable idea—as reasonable as any job opportunity that involved pimping and hooking could sound. After a few drinks and more talk, we decided to give it a try. We put an ad in the phone book, found ourselves a few women willing to work for us, and our brand-new escort service was in business.

One of the first people we added to our stable of escorts was a man I'd met at school. He didn't work for us as a man, however. He was a drag queen, and we sent him out on special calls for special clients. It was amazing to see the transformation from Bill to Bubbles. I often stared at him in fascination, astonished by the magic he performed with makeup, glamorous gowns, wigs, and well-rehearsed mannerisms.

I had long admired my mother's artistry with cosmetics—she was always flawless and beautiful. But this was a man, yet he was remarkably convincing as a woman. The entire transformation process appealed to my sense of theater. And when we sent "Bubbles" out as an escort, he never failed to be just exactly what the men who requested him were looking for.

Anne

Mary was amazing. From the instant I met her, I wanted her to be my best friend. Now that I was a Christian, I was looking for an intimate emotional relationship without a sexual dimension. I figured it was as close as I could get to a fulfilling relationship, and I assumed it would be all right with God.

Mary, too, was searching for intimacy. Like me, she was longing for a deep connection. She had no lesbianism in her background, but her desire for closeness drew her to me just as it drew me to her.

Mary lived off campus. She and a couple of roommates shared a neat old farmhouse where Campus Ambassadors often held 24-hour prayer meetings. Those were really happy times for all of us, and sometimes I spent the night there afterward as Mary and I talked into the wee hours of the morning.

At first I felt awkward about our sleeping arrangements, because I had lesbian feelings and a lesbian background. Yet, knowing my past, Mary allowed me to sleep in the same single bed, cuddled up with her. In our minds, there was no sexual contact, though it was inappropriately intimate, to say the least.

From time to time we wrote each other notes, gave each other flowers, and went through the whole romantic thing lovers do. I was soon deep into a relationship similar to all the other ones I'd ever had. I was powerfully attracted to yet another straight woman, caught in an unfulfilled attraction that both stimulated and frustrated my lesbian feelings.

"Look, Mary," I told her one day, just to make sure she understood, "we're getting pretty close. I'm really drawn to you. But if we ever engage in sexual activities, I'm just going to have to leave you. I don't want to lose my relationship with God."

I was convinced at that point that I could lose my salvation, that I could willingly walk away from God and He would let me go. I thought turning away from Him was the unforgivable sin. I was misinterpreting Scripture, but it was just as well. At the time, that's probably all that restrained me.

Meanwhile, my friend Lynn reentered my life. Although my birthday is in August, she waited until October to celebrate. "I want to take you out to a birthday dinner," she explained excitedly on the phone. "I want to celebrate your birthday and make it *special.*"

The evening of the celebration, she showed up with a beautiful card. She had flowers waiting for me at a romantic restaurant—a dozen yellow roses "for friendship," as she put it.

Despite my relationship with Mary, I still dreamed about Lynn. Yes, Lynn had always been the one for me. And Lynn had always been the one who refused to take things to the next level. But that night was different; there was no mistaking the change. Lynn looked beautiful. She was attentive and affectionate, and she was clearly romancing me. She had set in place all the elements a man would provide for his fiancée. We had a special intimate time talking about how we felt about each other. Oddly, in the midst of all that, I began to realize that I was in the woman's role and she was taking the male role. It was the first time that had ever happened to me.

After dinner, Lynn said, "Let's drive up by the beach." She drove us to a little park overlooking the ocean.

"I've got a blanket," she stated. "Let's sit and watch the stars a little."

My heart was pounding. But without hesitation, I went with her.

I had recently become a Christian. I'd committed myself to following Jesus regardless of my feelings. But here was the ultimate opportunity for me with Lynn, and in my view, she'd been in my life first, even before Jesus. Being with this woman had always been my dream—having sex with her and having her as a life partner. Now she was sitting wonderfully close to me while we talked, gazed at the stars, listened to the surf, and felt the wind on our faces.

"You know, I have this desire to kiss you," I said, half hoping she would answer, "Well, you know, Anne, maybe we shouldn't pursue this."

Instead she said, "Well, why don't you?"

This was the first time she had ever been open to an advance from me. Rather than pushing me away, she embraced me, and we began to caress each other. We didn't get far, though. Unexpectedly and suddenly, I had the most overwhelming sensation that Jesus knew exactly what I was doing. He could see perfectly well what was going on. He was watching. How could I betray Him after all He had done for me? It wasn't as if He were condemning me. Instead, I knew He was looking down on us and saying "Oh, Anne! Oh no, Anne!"

"Lynn," I said, pulling away, "I just can't do this. I've received so much from God, and I know this isn't the way to go. I would love to have sex with you and have you as my life partner, but it's not right and I can't do it."

In the aftermath, my emotional response was interesting. I actually felt a bit of joy after saying no, even though this was the

John was about a year old when this heartwarming picture with his father was taken.

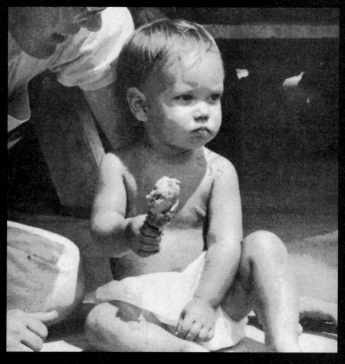

As a 1-year-old toddler, Anne was a typical, adorable little girl in a pretty dress.

Life seems great when you're three! Like most little boys, John loved taking a ride in his wagon.

Anne, at the innocent age of three, was shy but had a wonderful, tender personality.

John was a cute second-grader at the time his parents divorced.

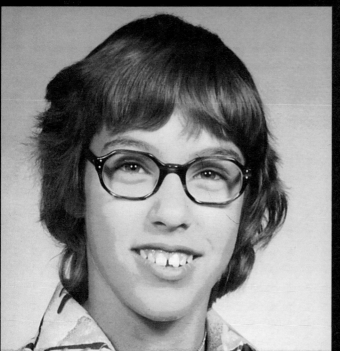

At age nine, Anne was looking more and more boyish.

In 1981, John was 18 years old and a senior in high school.

As a high school senior, Anne did not understand how wonderful it was to be a young woman.

At age 20 in college,
John's alter ego,
Candi, was born.

In college, Anne
relied on her
athletic ability
to feel good
about herself.

In 1988, at Love in Action, John felt happy and supported by other men who were also struggling to heal from homosexuality.

At Love in Action, Anne (pictured in the center) received the encouragement she needed to heal her gender identity.

At John's sister's wedding in 1990, he and his mother felt more bonded as a family than they had in many years.

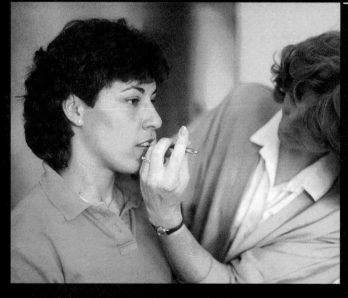

At age 25, Anne, with the help of her senior pastor's wife, tried on makeup for the first time.

July 19, 1992, was the happiest day for John and Anne!

John and Anne's
honeymoon in
Maui was like a
dream come true.

John and Anne,
at an Exodus
International con-
ference, met with
friends who have
also come out of
homosexuality.

On December 17, 1996, the Paulks' first son, Timothy Edward, was born.

Timmy enjoyed helping Anne decorate the Christmas tree in 1998. Anne was pregnant with the Paulks' second child, Alexander Gillett.

At one time, the
Paulks only
dreamed of the
kind of joy a
child could bring.
Timmy was a gift
from God.

The Paulks are pictured with Dr. James Dobson and Mike Trout
after they recorded a "Focus on the Family" broadcast.

John is pictured here at a Love Won Out conference he helped create for people concerned about the growing reality of homosexuality in youth.

This article from the August 17, 1998 issue of *Newsweek* featured the Paulks in their home.

Can Gays 'Convert'?

SOCIETY

A controversial series of ads claims that homosexuals aren't born that way, and can change the 'ex-gay' movement, and the elusive science of sexual orientation.

BY JOHN LELAND AND MARK MILLER

Fitting in, speaking
Ex-gays John and Anne Paulk minister to converting to ex-Exodus ministry, where they met. They married in 1992.

To the One who remembered us in our low estate
His love endures forever.
and freed us from our enemies,
His love endures forever.
and Who gives food to every creature.
His love endures forever.
Give thanks to the God of heaven.
His love endures forever.

—PSALM 136:23-26 (NIV)

ultimate relationship I had always dreamed about. But now I wanted something else. At the same time, I realized I had gained emotional independence from Lynn. She was no longer my reason for following Christ. I had my own relationship with Jesus now. The apron strings had been cut once and for all.

Later on, I tried to talk to Lynn about her relationship with the Lord. I had learned that she was getting involved with other women, and I was concerned about her. I met her down at the wharf one afternoon. "Look," I told her, "I'm a new Christian, but I'm afraid you're in jeopardy, and I'm just taking my biblical responsibility to call you to repent. That's all I'm asking for."

"Well, just give me some time," Lynn answered, and she left it at that. She has pursued a homosexual life ever since. For a long time afterward, I was devastated by her choices, but that didn't cause me to change my direction. Somehow, even though I wasn't doing everything perfectly, I had still managed to break free from Lynn.

John One afternoon, I was at Racine's house with Bill. He wasn't yet made up in drag, and we were both pretty bored and quiet. I noticed him staring at me, and it made me feel a little strange. I wasn't the least bit attracted to him in either persona.

"John," he said suddenly, "have you ever dressed in drag? You'd be so fabulous!"

I looked at him with what I hoped was an expression of utter disbelief.

"No, I'm serious, John," he insisted. "Your eyes are perfect for makeup. You've got the most feminine face. C'mon." He reached for his makeup case. "Let me try making you up. Let's have some fun."

"Bill, are you crazy?" I asked. "Believe me, a woman is the last thing I want to be!"

"Oh, lighten up, John," he challenged. "It'll be our little secret. What have you got to lose?"

"The rest of my self-respect—what's left of it," I mumbled, following him into the other room.

Bill acted as if he were a fine painter contemplating an empty canvas. He began with foundation and then painted and brushed and mascaraed and powdered and sculpted until I thought I would lose my mind.

"I feel like your fairy godmother," he cooed as he pinned back my hair and placed a cascade of black curls on my head.

I rolled my eyes, submitting to his obsessive efforts without a word. But when he was finished and held a mirror in front of me, I caught my breath in astonishment. I looked exactly like a woman—a dark-haired, sexy, Mediterranean beauty. Was the exotic female in the mirror really me?

Racine came back about then, and she was as amazed by the transformation as I was. The two of them rummaged through Racine's closet and began to outfit me in a gown, shoes, and the necessary underpinnings to make the dress look convincing.

In a few minutes, I had become someone new, someone glamorous, someone feminine and dramatic. That, in itself, was exciting. But even more appealing was the fact that, at least for the moment, I was no longer John Paulk. He was nowhere to be found.

Anne Mary couldn't have been more supportive while I was recovering from my encounter with Lynn. She came alongside me, exuding strength when I was feeling weak and broken. She comforted me emotionally and encouraged me spiritually.

I hadn't yet begun to realize that what went on between us was far too intimate. I was so unhealthy that I couldn't see how our relationship was unnatural and misguided. We were still sleeping together in a bed at times, but I perceived it as being "the best I can do." We might have been close to sin, I reasoned, but we weren't sinning. I couldn't see that I had made an idol out of Mary or that she was coming between Jesus and me.

When I was living at home and she was finishing her master's, she would take a Greyhound bus—even though she had practically no money—to come see me in Walnut Creek. I'd pick her up at the station, and she'd stay the weekend. We would spend the night in sleeping bags on my parents' living room floor. Once they went to bed, we'd cuddle up right next to each other, and we soon began to engage in more-intimate, almost sexual caresses. We were teetering on the edge of a huge chasm.

At about this time, a highly respected Christian publisher brought out a little book by a female author called *Homosexuality*. All she had to offer at the end of the book was, in so many words, "Grab onto your chair, make choices not to get yourself into vulnerable situations with other women, and grin and bear it for the rest of your life." That's all the hope I had, and that's what I was living out. It never occurred to me that my painful lesbian desires and longings could be removed.

Eventually Mary completed her master's program. Her great-grandparents had, at one time, been missionaries to China, and Mary had a heart filled with love for the Chinese. As a means of reaching Chinese students for Christ, she applied to a missions organization for a position in China and was accepted to become an English teacher. I was one of her references for getting that position.

Mary's last morning at my house was agonizing for both of us. We had slept out in the family room in sleeping bags to be close together, and we exchanged sad looks as we both got ready for the day.

"Mary," I told her, "before I take you to the airport, I want to give you something very special that I wrote for you."

As she read the framed poem about being best friends that I had written especially for her, her eyes filled with tears. "I have something for you too, Anne," she responded. Then she gave me her prized guitar as a parting gift.

"I … can't take this, Mary," I protested.

"Yes, you can. You have to take it. It's really important to me for you to have it."

The gesture touched me deeply because I knew that Mary had inherited it from her favorite aunt and it meant a great deal to her.

I tried to find words that could begin to express my deep feelings. "You're my best friend, Mary, and I can't even start to tell you how much I'm going to miss you. There will be an empty spot in my heart while you're away. I love you *so much.*"

Mary put her arms around me and held me close. "The same for me, my best buddy," she replied. "I love you more than you know, and I'll miss you incredibly."

We didn't say much more until it came time for her to board her plane. Once we were at the airport gate, words weren't enough. We just cried and held each other in a long good-bye bear hug.

"It will be hard, Anne, but let's try really hard to keep in touch," she said. "We can call occasionally. I'll send you my phone number as soon as I find out what it is. And I'll send you pictures. Please don't forget to tell me what's going on in your life and heart. I love you, my best friend."

And with that we parted. I stayed until the plane disappeared beyond the horizon and then headed for home, my face wet with tears.

John After celebrating my 21st birthday in wild, drug-crazed abandon, I found myself in the arms of a man I'd never known. I woke up early the next morning, wondering who he was and what my mother would think if she knew about my lifestyle. By now, I wasn't just John any more. I was Candi, a well-known drag queen in Columbus.

What would Mom say if she found out? What would she do if I told her?

My opportunity came soon enough. My therapist, Brian, had been encouraging me to tell my mom I was gay. So had Ron, my latest boyfriend. I certainly wasn't looking forward to it, though; what would I do if my mom rejected me? But at Ron's prodding, I agreed to go out to dinner with him and my mom.

At the restaurant, Mom remarked that I was now old enough to order hard liquor. Could she really be so unaware of who I was and what I did? My drinking was so heavy and habitual that even I worried about it sometimes.

As the evening wound down, I continued to hesitate, wondering if it wouldn't be better to wait just another day or two or three. But Ron wasn't going to wait another minute. "Isn't there something you have to say to your mother, John?" he prompted late in the dinner.

My mother turned her lovely eyes my way, and I choked out, "Uh, yeah. I guess there is."

"John, is everything all right?" she asked. Her face looked troubled. She was probably thinking the worst; but was her worst fear as bad as what I was about to tell her?

"Mom, I ... You may have ..." I stopped, tried to form a coherent sentence, then simply said, "I'm gay, Mom. I guess I want you to know the real me, and that's who I really am."

Her eyes fixed on mine, and she looked as calm and poised as ever. "Well of course you are, John," she replied. "I've known that for ages. I never said anything because I didn't want to intrude. I knew you'd let me know when the time was right for you."

A tide of relief washed over me. It was done, and Mom wasn't angry, hurt, or horrified. In fact, she was virtually unmoved by the entire revelation. Her demeanor gave me the courage to ask the question that had terrified me every time I envisioned myself telling her. "So what do you think about this, Mom? How do you feel?"

"John, you're my only son," she answered. "I can't imagine anything that would keep me from loving you just as much as I always have. Being gay is a lonely way of life, and I hope you aren't going to suffer too much because of it. I guess that makes me wish things were different, but as far as loving you is concerned, nothing could ever change that. Not in a million years, John."

The relief I felt was warm and comforting. I knew that in the future I would be more at ease around her and more able to open up about my life. But there were still two things I vowed she'd never learn. I wouldn't tell her about the escort service, and I couldn't bear the thought of her knowing I was Candi, Columbus's drag queen extraordinaire.

Anne
✎

Without Mary to lean on, I longed to recapture the wonderful Christian nurturing I'd experienced with Campus Ambassadors. But Cal State Hayward was a commuter school, and the atmosphere was less friendly and comfortable than U.C. Santa Barbara had been. Campus Crusade for Christ had a presence there, but they focused on evangelism, and I wasn't really interested in that. Fortunately, at about that time, InterVarsity college ministry brought a woman to the Hayward campus to start up a Christian fellowship.

I immediately revealed my struggle to her and told her what kind of support I thought I needed. Together, we started organizing a group. And at our first meeting, I met a girl named Melissa who was a freshman at Mills College, a nearby women's school. From what she told me, about a third of the women at Mills were lesbians.

Melissa had a butch haircut with a tail in the back, but she was more feminine in nature than I was. I began to look after her, thinking of myself as her big sister. Little by little, the two of us developed a friendship. Nothing emotionally inappropriate happened, at least not at first. I was still caught up in Mary, and no one could compare to her.

Melissa was both interesting and interested, however, and I was soon to learn that she was more than a little jealous of Mary.

John My sister, Vicky, was getting ready to graduate from high school in Portland, Oregon. I knew that if I attended her graduation, Dad would be there, too. I hadn't seen him for years.

I flew to Portland with Mom and my grandmother. There we met up with Dad, who was still struggling with depression himself after his divorce from Ellen, his second wife. I had no idea what to expect when I saw him and wasn't sure he even wanted to see me. My feelings of alienation from him had intensified in recent years, and I wasn't looking forward to our meeting, simply because I thought he might reject me once and for all.

But we all had at least one thing in common—we were all tremendously proud of Vicky. Not only was she valedictorian of her class, but she had been accepted at Georgetown University as well. Tears brimmed in my eyes as she marched in wearing her cap and gown. And it was a great moment for our family to hear her speech, in which she so eloquently reflected upon the future and shared her vision for her graduating class.

A few days later, just before my return flight to Columbus, Dad and I were spending some time together in his apartment. He was warm and friendly, and I was relieved to be sitting around comfortably with him, looking at old family photos and remembering my childhood. As always, I felt a longing in my heart to be closer to Dad.

Later on, as we stood at the airport check-in counter, I was struggling with my emotions. "You're coming to the gate with me, aren't you, Dad?" I asked. I didn't want to leave him.

"I can't do it, John," he replied. His voice broke, and he looked away from me. "I have a hard time saying good-bye, son. If you don't mind, I'll just leave you here." With that, he gave me a big hug and held me longer than I expected. Both of us were in tears as he went his way and I went mine, each of us feeling profoundly alone.

Some months later, I received a letter from him that began to rebuild some of the broken places in my heart. It read:

> Dear John,
>
> For a long time there has been an unspoken tension between us. Some of this was bound to arise, since neither of us has made much effort to maintain communication. I'm making an effort to change that from my end. If there are other reasons on your part, I would like to see them slip away.
>
> If part of the problem is that you think I don't care, then put that feeling aside. I do care. You are carrying a burden, because you have not chosen to tell me that you are gay. And I would like to address that.
>
> It is not necessary for a son to have approval from a father to be able to go forward with life. What does make a difference is that two people accept each other, with individual rights, ambitions, and choices.
>
> I accept you as an individual. You are your own man. But you are still my son. All I ask is your acceptance in return. We don't have to be the same kind of men to love each other. I love you. Don't let bitterness about your life interfere with living it.
>
> Love,
> Dad

Anne Mary's absence had opened a huge hole in my life, and Melissa instinctively tried to fill it. At first I was almost inconsolable in my grief, but I tried to keep moving forward, clinging to my faith for dear life. I was still involved in all sorts of Christian activities, Bible studies, and social events. Everybody looked up to me because

I had such a commitment to God. But the truth was that, although they couldn't see it, I was really an emotional mess.

Melissa also had a real relationship with Christ, but she lacked close friendships and was looking for someone to attach to on a human level. Because she was so affectionate and so devoted to me, gradually she began to fill the void that Mary had left. She was successful to a point, but no one could have filled Mary's shoes completely—at least not yet.

Despite some endearing times we enjoyed together, Melissa was becoming increasingly jealous. We had known each other for almost a year, and she longed to be closer to me. I understood very well how she felt—how many times had I experienced the same frustration? I watched as she competed for my attention. She did everything she could to gain my favor. And it should have been easy—the one she was competing with was thousands of miles away.

John No matter how exciting the pleasures of my life became, no matter how wild the nights or how frenzied the excitement, everything I did was acted out against a backdrop of depression and despair. I couldn't keep relationships together. I couldn't achieve the success I longed for. I could barely stand the sight of myself in the mirror. Feelings of self-loathing haunted me, and only alcohol and sex seemed to keep them at bay.

One night, even my usual forms of "anesthesia" weren't enough. I looked at myself in the bathroom mirror and snarled at my reflection, "I hate you! I hate everything about you!"

I grabbed a bottle of scotch and downed it without bothering with ice or a glass. As the burning sensation inflamed my throat, I welcomed the thick haze that began to cloud my mind. Suddenly, driven by some diabolical impulse, I went to the medicine cabinet, grabbed a bottle of pain pills, and poured them out into my hand. For a moment I stared at the pills, drunkenly admiring their shiny red color. Then without calculation or hesitation, yearning to end my agony once and for all, I tossed them into my mouth and washed them down with more scotch.

I then stretched out across the couch for what I hoped would be my last, final sleep. But just as my eyes closed, I was startled awake by a voice in my mind. "John," the voice said, "you don't want to die. What you really want is to be rescued. You need someone to help you, someone to love and care for you."

Reluctantly, I responded. Incoherent as I was, I somehow managed to call a suicide hotline. And out of our garbled conversation, the counselor was able to extract Dr. Brian Taylor's name from me. Soon Brian called in response to the counselor's message. After talking with me for a while, and after checking on the pain medication I had taken, he was able to determine that I hadn't ingested a harmful dose of pills after all, even considering the amount of scotch I had drunk.

In the counseling sessions that followed, Brian became more and more convinced that if I didn't deal with my alcohol abuse problem, there wasn't much more he could do to help me.

"So you think I'm an alcoholic?" I asked Brian, my voice edgy and defensive. "Is that what you're trying to say?"

"Are you saying you aren't?" he challenged. "Look at the facts, John. You drink habitually, and sometimes you drink until you pass out. Those are clear warning signs."

"Alcoholics can't stop drinking, Brian. You know that. But I can stop if I want to. I just don't want to right now."

"That's the point. You don't want to because you can't!"

"Brian, I don't because I'm not interested in stopping. Look, you're just trying to label me an alcoholic because you're worried about my suicide attempt. It's not going to happen again, so you can relax. I was just upset."

Brian looked at me with a calm, reasonable expression. "John, until you get help with your alcohol abuse issues, my hands are tied. Alcohol is getting in the way of your growth."

"You're overreacting, Brian," I insisted. "It's not a problem. Trust me."

Brian wasn't the least bit convinced by my denial. He knew an addict when he saw one.

One Saturday night several weeks later, I was both drunk and snorting poppers at the "K." I was in drag, having the time of my life, dancing the night away as Candi, without a care in the world. Then for some reason I glanced upward, and my eyes were suddenly transfixed by a mirror ball that was rotating slowly near the ceiling. I smiled as I watched the intricate patterns of light swirling across the ceiling and walls.

Suddenly, all at once, I seemed to enter another place and time. The frenzied reality of the club instantly ceased. The music stilled, and I could no longer hear the thumping of the beat. Everything was suspended. And in the silence that seemed to have fallen like a curtain around me, I heard a voice again. It wasn't audible in the physical sense, but it resounded loud and clear in my mind.

"Come back to Me," the voice said, "and I will change your life."

I immediately recognized it as the voice of God. "Come back to Me," He repeated.

I answered silently in my mind, *But I don't know how to get back to You. How can I do that? I'm so far away.*

In that instant, the music came back and the suspension of reality was broken. But my heart was filled with a yearning for this pure connection I had unmistakably made. The voice had been so loving, so benevolent.

As I left the dance floor abruptly to get another drink, my thoughts carried me back to when I was 15 and the conversation I'd had with my friend Clara. I remembered kneeling at my window after that talk, asking Jesus to come into my life. My heart welled with emotion, and I suddenly longed to be 15 again.

When the bartender handed me my scotch on the rocks, however, the entire experience evaporated. Once again I was Candi, a vision of loveliness on the dance floor, determined to party the night away.

Anne   Melissa's dormitory at Mills College was full of
              lesbians, and many of them lived on her floor.
              Since the attraction between Melissa and me was
ever increasing and we could hardly keep our hands off each
other, we fit in pretty well.

To my amazement, Melissa wasn't the only one interested in
me. Several of the lesbians in the dorm were also checking me
out, and some actually told me they found me very attractive. I
was taking judo lessons at the time, and one night I was demon-
strating a move to them. One of the women had short-cropped,
black hair and wore unisex clothing. She caught my attention
because of her masculine mannerisms, and I decided to use her
for my demonstration.

I grabbed her and placed her in a judo position. As I held
her, she looked me directly in the eyes and said, "You know, I
really like you."

I was surprised. I would never have imagined that three or
four women could be interested in me at the same time. Still, it
was obvious that they all wanted something, and that "something" was unmistakably sexual.

That night, Melissa found out about the others, too. She
had already been trying to turn my thoughts away from
Mary. Now she felt even more driven, and the sense of com-
petition enhanced the unfulfilled sexual element in our relationship.

Melissa probably thought, *If we had sex, that would be our special connection. Then we'd be together for good.* But I still wasn't
really over Mary, and the time was growing closer when I
would see her again.

Somehow, we both resisted temptation. I thought we could
go on forever without crossing the line into sexual intimacy. I
believed that my faith would see us through. And since I never
imagined anything weakening my faith, I had no idea how vulnerable I really was.

John   Columbus's Miss Ingenue contest pitted the city's
~~~~   most notorious drag queens against each other,
           and in 1985, I was very much in the running. But
after an alcohol-fogged performance at the contest, and after
failing to be crowned Miss Ingenue, my dissatisfaction with
myself and my life continued to eat away at me.

I was drinking very heavily by now, and in our therapy sessions, Brian and I began to take a closer look at Candi and what
she represented in my life. He tried to help me see that I was
hiding from myself when I was Candi. I heard his words, but I
wasn't able to grasp everything he was saying, even though I
knew it made a great deal of sense.

As if losing the contest and hating my life weren't enough, I
also became infuriated with my mother for breaking up with
her latest boyfriend, who had befriended me and was learning
to love me. One night, in a state of frustration and rage, I got so
drunk that I didn't know what I was doing. I went out cruising
the gay bars, looking for any and every distraction I could find.
Several potential lovers tried to pick me up, but one particular
man was more persistent than the others.

I went to my apartment with him, and after a few more
drinks, I blacked out. When I finally woke up, there was blood
all over my bed, and it was obvious that I had been cruelly
abused. I was in great pain, not only from a severe hangover, but
also from the condition of my body. Somehow in the night
when I was beyond consciousness, I had been brutally raped. I
had also been robbed, losing a family heirloom ring as well as
all my cash.

As painful as the rape was both physically and financially, the
greatest toll it took on me was emotional. As many times as I had
subjected myself to unwelcome sexual activities, never before had
I been violated like that—violently and against my will. My head
throbbed with pain, nausea lingered all the next day, and I
vomited several times. No matter what I did, I couldn't shake off
the horrible sense of defilement that I felt.

When Brian heard what had happened, he confronted me about my drinking once again. "I've worked with you for quite a while, John, and you've made some great progress. But there's nothing more we can do until you get a handle on your alcohol problem," he said firmly. "I want you to check out Drummers. It's a gay Alcoholics Anonymous group. You need their help and you need it *now*, John. In fact, I hate to say this, but until you've attended at least one of their meetings, I'm not going to see you again."

"Oh, c'mon, Brian," I protested. "You're—"

"John," Brian interrupted, his mind clearly made up, "either go to the Drummers or don't bother to come back."

I wasn't the least bit excited about attending. But to my surprise, when I stepped into St. Mary's Catholic Church where the Drummers group was meeting, I recognized some people and realized that I wasn't going to be as out of place—and anonymous—as I'd imagined. As the first meeting progressed, I allowed my eyes to scan the room, and I was pleased to notice that there were some attractive gay men there. Maybe things weren't going to be so bad after all.

During the meeting, as with all AA groups, people told about their experiences with alcohol—their powerlessness, their out-of-control lives, their inability to stop drinking on their own. I understood exactly what they were talking about.

I couldn't hide from the truth any longer. When the man in charge said, "No one can decide whether you're an alcoholic but you," I was ready to make a painful admission. *Yes*, I silently assented, *my name is John, and I'm an alcoholic.*

Alcoholics Anonymous people talk a lot about serenity, and it shows in their lives. They also talk often about "the Higher Power," or "God, as you understand Him to be." I hadn't thought much about God before—apart from the strange incident on the dance floor and my brief flirtation with Christianity in high school—but I could see that these people really were God-conscious.

"It's the power of God that keeps us sober and restores us to sanity," they'd often say sincerely. "You need to get in touch with your Higher Power," they'd encourage me. "You've got to learn to rely on something bigger than yourself."

Anne Summer arrived, and with it came my college graduation and a hard-earned degree in physical education. What better way could I celebrate than to be reunited with Mary? It was a dream come true for me to travel to China and visit her for about six weeks. I was overwhelmed with excitement and anticipation. Mary and I were going to be together again!

However, it didn't take me more than a couple of days with Mary to discover that she had developed a close relationship with a Chinese national, a woman named Han. I found it unbelievable that she could have already attached herself to someone else just as closely as she had been attached to me. I don't know which was the stronger emotion, my jealousy or my deep sense of abandonment.

I was devastated. I had looked forward to that trip for months, imagining that Mary and I would recapture the wonderful aspects of our friendship. But from the moment I arrived, it couldn't have been more clear: Things between us would never be the same as they once were. After a few days of relentless disappointment, feeling battered and broken, I left Mary early and rejoined the mission group that I would be traveling with for the duration of my trip.

The more I thought about it, the more I blamed God. As far as I was concerned, He had yanked the rug out from under my feet emotionally. How could He have allowed us to become so close and then let her establish the same kind of relationship with this other woman? My whole world was turned upside down. Because I had never seen my relationship with Mary for what it really was, I couldn't comprehend God's purposes in allowing it to end. Instead, I raged against Him.

I was there as a youth missionary, intending to help others come to Jesus. Instead, for the rest of the trip I had little to offer anyone else. I was lost in grief over what felt like a double betrayal—both Mary and God had forsaken me. The other girls saw that I was hurting and were kind to me. At times they would come up to me, put their arms around me, and try to get me to talk.

I told them as much as I could. I explained that a close friendship apparently hadn't been as close as I'd thought. Those faithful young women really came alongside me. They sympathized with me. They prayed with me. All of them were straight and I was trying to overcome lesbianism, but that didn't matter to them. They were there when I needed them, and they were incredibly loving and kind.

John

After several months of sobriety, my life began to change. Instead of being irresponsible and untrustworthy, I was keeping a steady job at a campus print shop and got a promotion to manage my own store. Instead of having memory gaps and blackouts, I was able to remember the events from the previous night when I woke up in the morning. Instead of reaching for a drink every time I felt the urge, I learned to distract myself until the cravings passed.

I saw the serenity in the AA people at Drummers, and my thoughts sometimes turned to the "Higher Power" they talked about. Because of my new clarity of mind, I learned to be more honest. After relating my progress to Mom, to my amazement, she started to attend AA meetings herself. Before long, she begrudgingly admitted that she, too, was an alcoholic. The only surprise to me was that she admitted it.

Even Candi was changing. She wasn't as wild and cruel as she had once been, and although her one-liners were still hilarious, they were more clever than cutting.

I still hadn't told Dad about my drinking problem. Gathering my courage, I wrote him a letter and explained that I was in recovery and had been sober for seven months. Not long afterward, I received this reply:

> *John, it was a fine gesture on your part to disclose your alcoholism to me. It is understandable that my not mentioning anything before could lead you to think that I was either shocked or, for some reason, did not know how to deal with the situation.*
>
> *In fact, I was concerned in my last letter that you know how proud I am of how you are trying to work through things rather than highlighting the obstacles you have faced. John, nothing in life shocks or even really surprises me. There is little I have not been exposed to. I'm very aware of the human condition.*
>
> *I do not mean to sound like I am downplaying the problem of alcoholism. It is real and does not just go away. Some people are more susceptible than others. Whether this is due to allergies, chemical reactions, or social dysfunction is not important. If alcohol is wrong for you, then you are fortunate to recognize it and darn lucky to take steps to protect yourself.*
>
> *John, all my love and best wishes to you. Life is a long time. Find out what is important for you and grow in the joy.*
>
> *Love you, Dad*

Several incidents followed that letter in rapid sequence. First, I met Matt. He was a gorgeous blond man who caught my eye while I was Candi. I soon learned that Candi had turned his head more than once over the past year. He wanted to take pictures of me, and I was more than happy to oblige him. He gave me his phone number, and I promised to call.

After a couple of false starts, Matt and I finally got together, and I started to think something special was about to happen between us. We had such a great time together—we loved the same movies, the same music, and the same food. Even more interestingly, Matt seemed to appreciate John as much as he admired Candi. In fact, he made a point of calling me John even when I was in drag.

Shortly after I met Matt, another friend made a very interesting comment. One night, he walked up to me at a bar and said, "John, just look at how popular Candi has become. Have you ever wondered what would happen if you acted like Candi while still dressed as John? I bet the whole world would love you."

His comments started me thinking about my reasons for dressing as Candi. I acted like a completely different person when I was in drag. I felt confident, popular, and accepted. But could it be, I thought, that Candi was just an expression of my own personality? She was a costume, a mask—a crutch, really. Maybe I didn't need her image to hide behind after all.

This was a new thought, however, and I wasn't yet ready to be done with Candi. I still intended, for one thing, to appear as Candi at that year's Gay Pride Day parade. Matt rented a red Mustang convertible for the occasion and decorated it with crepe paper, streamers, and balloons. He wore a white tuxedo to chauffeur me as I rode in the back. Goodale Park was the starting point, and in the festive spirit of the day, lots of people told us how good we looked. Thousands of people were taking part; the parade would be several miles long.

The Stonewall Union, the local gay activist group, had assigned two tough-looking lesbian guards with armbands to walk alongside our car during the parade in case there were any protesters. Things went well at first, with bystanders calling out to me, "You're the queen of queens!" while I tossed starlight mints into the crowd. As we approached the bridge over the Olentangy River, however, we heard chanting. An eerie feeling crept over me; my spine tingled, and I grew scared.

Soon the parade came to a temporary stop, and I found myself stuck in the middle of a group of angry Christian protesters. Many of them held signs that bore Scripture quotations or phrases like "Turn or burn!" with orange flames. Some in the crowd were screaming, some were weeping, and others were praying with bowed heads. I recognized one of the people as a trainer from my health club who was usually nice to me. *How can he be part of this group?* I wondered. *And why can't these people just leave us alone?*

"Why are these people bothering us?" I asked Matt. I suddenly felt small and condemned, as if God really did hate me.

Our guards remained calm through all this. "Don't talk to them!" they urged. "Don't even look at them. They're idiots. Behave better than them." I felt safe with those guards protecting us, and before long the parade started moving again.

No matter what I said or thought, however, those Christians made me feel dirty and ashamed. I hated them for it. What right did they have to impose their self-righteousness on me?

Fortunately, that unpleasant encounter ended without incident. But it was followed just days later by another one. After I made a flamboyant appearance at a club, a straight man tried to hit on Candi, and I was revolted by the entire situation. For some reason, his lecherous attention was the last straw for me.

For several months, the thrill of appearing in drag had been diminishing. It was no longer exciting, and the lengthy process of transforming myself into another person of another sex—even a stunningly beautiful one—had become boring. As I grew more in touch with John, I became more disassociated with my alter ego. I had proved to myself that I could be a convincingly glamourous woman, and there was no more challenge involved. Besides, I was beginning to resent the attention men paid to Candi without knowing or caring anything about John.

For any number of reasons, some of which I didn't even understand at the time, I was sick and tired of Candi. I was even more sick and tired of the entire drag game and weary beyond words of having to live with a split identity.

In a frenzy of determination, I loaded four years of Candi's wardrobe and makeup into a large box and hurled the whole mess into a Dumpster. Candi was gone, and I felt as if I had been released from a cold, dark prison.

Some of my friends were shocked, especially those who had been in drag with me. "You can't just dump Candi like a piece of baggage, John," they argued. "Candi's part of you! You'll never be the same without her!"

"You're wrong," I said. "I don't need Candi anymore. She's *not* me—and I'll never do drag again as long as I live."

Anne After that trip to China, I remained bitter toward God. I thought He had tricked and betrayed me. In response, I stopped talking to Him for a year. That estrangement left me open to act however I wanted, without consulting or obeying Him.

It's not surprising that during that year, Melissa and I steadily increased our expressions of physical affection. We began to say good-bye with huge bear hugs. As everybody left a gathering or meeting, she and I would be the last to go, sharing the longest hug. I could feel the sexual tension between us, and I knew it was mutual. But we still weren't acting on it.

Then one night, Melissa and I were staying in the same room at a friend's house. Melissa was on the floor; I was on the bed. I leaned over and gave her a little good-night hug.

"The heck with it," she said quietly and began to kiss me on the lips. Next she pulled me over on top of her. In the moments that followed, we initiated our long-awaited sexual relationship. And from then on, she became sexually attached to me, even to the point of making sexual moves when we were with other people. To our friends it looked like playful teasing and touching. But the truth was we were having a lesbian relationship right under their noses. I enjoyed it immensely, but I was often embarrassed.

So it was that, after all the emotional ups and downs, after dancing around the possibilities for years, I was finally involved in my first real lesbian sexual relationship. And, for a little while, I was thrilled. I don't think Melissa and I even considered changing our behavior for at least a month. I felt no conviction whatsoever. In fact, I thought we were living a dual life fairly well. It was true—no one seemed to notice.

All my childhood dreams had suddenly come true, yet it was even better than that. I was a woman, and I wasn't pretending to be a man. The sex was great as far as feelings of stimulation and fulfillment were concerned. But we were playing a game, hiding the truth from other people, and eventually that took its toll. All the secrecy began to remind us that we were doing something that contradicted what we believed. Our moral standards were being compromised to accommodate our feelings.

Since we were now doing everything together, I attended church with her as well. Melissa's church believed in using prophetic gifts, and every time I walked through the door I was terrified that God would somehow open up the whole sky and say, in front of hundreds of people, "Anne, you're involved in a lesbian sexual relationship!"

Deep inside, I knew God wouldn't do that, but I became paranoid anyway. I was ready to pull the plug and run in order to appease my guilty conscience. Maybe if I stopped seeing Melissa, I thought, I would no longer be tempted by lesbian sex. So more and more frequently I told her, "Look, we really need to break this off."

One time when I said that, she threatened to commit suicide. She tried to manipulate me because she was afraid of losing me.

Instead of breaking up, Melissa and I began a process of resisting, then giving in, then resisting again. But our resistance wasn't very strong. Our feelings and our physical desires took charge every time. My flesh wanted satisfaction; my heart wanted Melissa. It was a heavy, hopeless battle.

In retrospect, I can see that if I hadn't found myself in that no-win situation with Melissa, I never would have found real healing. In that futile attempt to do right, I was deeply humbled. Failure knocked me off my lofty throne and removed once and for all the illusion that I was handling everything properly, keeping a lid on my sexuality while continuing to toy with lesbian emotions.

At last I came to see that I hadn't dealt with any of the issues that drew me toward women. There were any number of aspects of my gender confusion about which I needed to ask for and accept other people's help. Until that summer, when I finally fell prey to my own desires, I hadn't looked for answers. My troubles weren't going to be solved through Bible study and prayer alone. My problem was deeper than I'd thought. It was unmanageable. Lesbianism was no longer a pattern of thought or behavior that I could control.

During those months, I became aware of one wonderful truth: God doesn't desert a person who is acting in habitual sin. He continued to deal with me on a deep level, even in the midst of my sin. At the end of four months of sexual activity with Melissa, I said, *God, I love this sin. I love this sin. It feels so fulfilling. There's no way, if it's offered to me, that I can turn it down now. I know. I've tasted it, and I think it's awesome. It's the fulfillment of all my dreams. It's an addiction. I can't say no. There's no more fight in me for that. You are going to have to do something. I want You to be the first love of my life, and I know You aren't right now. You're going to have to change my heart. You're just going to have to make the changes for me.*

And that's just what He did. A couple of days later, I was in Melissa's room, talking on the phone with my InterVarsity leader. She was chatting away, trying to explain some kind of new thinking about relationships and Christian fellowship that she'd been learning. I think it must have been a new strategy for outreach.

Because of my guilt, however, I thought she was pointing her finger at me. Assuming she already knew, I told her all about my relationship with Melissa. I started by saying, "I'll bet you're saying this because Melissa and I are ..." and I went on from there.

The poor woman was clueless. She'd had no idea. There was a silence on the other end of the line as she listened and allowed me to talk. And then she was discerning enough to ask me questions. By the end of that phone call, she had the whole story.

When Melissa came in, I said, "You know, I just spilled the beans about us."

"You what?" she exclaimed. "Now we're in big trouble! We're not going to be able to get away with this, you know."

Though I didn't see it at the time, God had caused me to do this in answer to my own prayer, which had been an honest prayer—a real heart's cry.

Melissa and I soon met with some InterVarsity leaders who were firm in their response: "You two need to give up your relationship immediately. Put it in God's hands. He may restore it in the future in some new, healthy form, but you have absolutely no claim on it now."

The anger with God that I'd felt about losing Mary was stirred up again. Emotionally, Melissa had become what Mary had been to me, and now I was losing her, too. After that meeting, I rushed outside. My car was parked beside a lake, and I threw my keys up as high as I could into the night sky, not knowing if they would land in the lake or if I'd ever find them again.

Quickly realizing how foolish I'd been, I started searching for my keys. Finally I found them and got into my car. I wept inconsolably. I prayed, *God, it's happened again—she's the only one who really knows me. And once again, I'm losing the person who really understands me, the very love I was looking for!*

That was the end of my relationship with Melissa, and that was the beginning of my healing; I was about to become a new person. I was also about to find a whole new group of friends and supporters who would help me through. But change doesn't come easily. At least for me, it certainly didn't happen overnight.

Love
in Action

John

The escort service Racine and I had launched never really got off the ground, and during the day I continued to manage the campus print shop, where business was boring but stable and I didn't have the vice squad or sexually transmitted diseases as occupational hazards. I soon got to know a number of regular customers on a first-name basis, and one couple in particular captured my attention.

Tom and Denise Walters had a ministry at Ohio State, so I assumed they were religious. But they were fun to talk to, and I always enjoyed seeing them when they came into the shop. Then, in a series of what seemed like coincidences, I kept seeing them when I wasn't working at the shop. Little by little, the three of us became friends, and it was an odd friendship. They were conservative, I was flamboyantly gay, yet they genuinely seemed to like me. When I was sick, they brought me food. When I was down, they encouraged me. I was drawn to them in an unexplainable way. But all the while, a small, yellow light kept flashing in the back of my mind, warning me that they had some sort of intentions that didn't involve photocopies.

One afternoon, Tom asked if he could come to my apartment. "There's something I'd like to talk to you about," he said.

"What is it?" I asked, my eyes narrowing in suspicion. "Why can't we talk about it here?" I knew well how Christians felt about gays, and all my defenses were on full alert. I figured he wanted to give me the "big conversion speech." So why did I agree to have Tom visit me at home? I really had no idea.

When he knocked on my door later that day, I thought about pretending I wasn't home. I was busy making my usual lavish Valentine's Day cards for all my gay friends. But I decided after a minute to let him into my apartment filled with gay-oriented posters and photos, and he immediately pulled out a big, black Bible.

Starting in the book of John, he began talking about God's love for everyone and the deity of Jesus and how we all need a Savior, someone to pick up the pieces of our broken lives for us. Though Tom spoke generally about how we all do wrong things, my thoughts turned instantly to my gay behavior.

"Tom," I said, "I'm gay, so God can't love me."

Tom started laughing. "Who told you that?" he asked. "Not only *could* He love you, but He *does* love you."

I told him about my conversion at age 15 and then said, "All I want to know is, if I die right now, will I go to heaven?"

"Yes," he answered. "You've been a Christian all these years. But that's only part of the story. It's one thing to give your life to God," he answered. "It's another thing to live a life that's pleasing to Him. You may go to heaven, but you'll have nothing to show for your life, no reward. If you love God, you will obey Him." He showed me in his Bible passages like 1 John 2 that make that point, as well as others like Romans 8 that affirm God's undying love for us.

I suddenly realized that I *did* believe the tenets of Christianity. I did believe I was sinful and in need of forgiveness; I had just pushed it all down into my subconscious for years, allowing myself to be brainwashed by the gay lifestyle and rhetoric. Now I felt *guilty*.

As Tom spoke, I knew that I did love God. Through the love and grace Tom and Denise had shown me over the past months, I had seen Christian love lived out, and I felt a deep love for God in return. I found it a stunning revelation.

"Can I have a lover and still be a Christian?" I asked next.

"I can't answer that for you," Tom replied. "All I know is that God would not be pleased with your life." Then he showed me various passages in the Bible that talk about homosexuality. After that, he left.

Over the next few days, I thought again about Clara and the decision I'd made to accept Jesus while I was in high school. I thought about the "Higher Power" in AA and how that Power seemed to have helped me when I didn't have the strength to help myself.

I also recalled the strange thought that had come into my mind while I was dancing at the "K": *I want you to come back to Me. I can free you from all this and change your life.*

One night as I pondered these things, tears flooded my eyes and poured down my face. Could this somehow be the answer I'd been looking for? Impulsively, I knelt by my bed, hoping that something wonderful was about to happen.

Lord, I prayed, *I don't know what You have in mind. I don't know how to stop being homosexual or if that's even possible. But I want to give my life back to You. If You'll help me, I'll trust You and never turn away from You again.*

The date was February 10, 1987, and I was 23 years old.

Anne

My entanglement with Melissa wasn't easily put away. Now that I had sexual experiences to recall, it was far more difficult to stop dwelling on my times with her than it had been with Mary. I had flashbacks, and I was sexually aroused simply by thinking about them. But my desire to obey God was strong, and I was determined to do all I could to overcome my impulses.

I was grateful for my Bible study group at church and for the Exodus ministry gatherings where I could be really honest. I felt a great deal of support from those around me—people who listened and encouraged me. Their support upheld my desire to follow Jesus out of all the confusion between my sexual and my spiritual desires. For the first time in my life, I knew I didn't have all the answers. I recognized that I really needed the help and prayers of others. And by now, I was humble enough to ask.

Sometimes as I was driving, a sexual memory would flash

into my mind, and I would start to experience a sexual response before I'd even had time to think about it. So I'd look out the car window and say something like, "Gosh, Lord, there's a tree out there! That tree is green, and it has leaves on it. It's got brown bark." I would fix my mind on anything and everything I could find to distract myself.

Because my feelings were so consuming and so addictive, I needed to attack my obsession about Melissa with severity. I had to monitor every thought, and I had to do it for months. Dangerous ideas came at me uninvited and unexpected. And even though Melissa and I were no longer involved, I still had to stop dwelling on the memories.

Over time, that process made me mentally disciplined enough to displace all lesbian thoughts, period. It amounted to bringing every thought captive to the obedience of Christ every second of every day. I didn't know it then, but I was following a biblical instruction at a very practical level.

As helpful as the Exodus ministry proved to be to me, it's ironic that I attended my first Exodus meeting only because I had no other choice. It happened shortly before Melissa and I broke up, when we were trying without success to return our relationship to a nonsexual level.

Melissa had heard of a woman named Sheila Hanson, a therapist who attended an Exodus group in San Rafael. So Melissa and I went there one night and met her for dinner. We told her we wanted to retain our relationship but take the sex out of it. She smiled knowingly, well aware that it wasn't going to work. As she listened to us, I'm sure she could see all sorts of patterns revealing themselves. But she knew we couldn't handle much, so she simply encouraged us to follow God.

After dinner, we followed Sheila outside the restaurant. I was expecting to say good-bye, but Sheila spoke up first. "Melissa, you can follow my car to the house where our group meets," she said. "It's not far."

I looked at Melissa with angry consternation on my face, a

look that clearly meant, "What does she mean 'group'? *What group?*"

Melissa ignored my reaction and told Sheila, "Sure, I'm driving a yellow VW. I'll wait for your car at the corner."

As we walked to Melissa's Bug, we got into a heated discussion. I was furious. "What do you think you're doing?" I demanded. "You know I hate therapy groups, Melissa. I don't want to go, but now I'm stuck since you drove us here. I'm over an hour away from home. I hate this!"

Melissa was nonchalant. "I know you don't like these meetings, but let's just go tonight and see what it's like," she suggested. "It can't hurt too much to go to one meeting."

We drove the rest of the way in silence. The minute we walked in the door, everyone in the room knew exactly what Melissa and I were dealing with.

At Exodus, I saw people who faced the same struggles I did, yet they were changing. I was attracted to them, drawn to return again and again. Melissa, on the other hand, went just one more time.

It was a couple of weeks later that Melissa and I broke up after being confronted by our ministry leaders. But following that first Exodus meeting, I knew I had a place to go for help, and I wasn't alone in my struggle. The group supported me because every person there understood where I was coming from. At one time or another, they had all experienced feelings like mine, and they had made it through. I started really investing myself in this drop-in meeting every Friday night. I had to drive an hour and 10 minutes to get there, but I committed myself to being present every week. Somehow, in all my confusion, I knew they had the answers I so desperately needed.

John
〜

Was it possible to be a gay Christian? I still felt the same gay feelings I'd always had. My soul may have been saved, but I didn't see any other changes. And I didn't know what to do about it.

Denise and Tom continued to pray for me, love me, and encourage me to read my Bible. I tried to talk to some of the AA people about whether someone could be a Christian and continue in the gay lifestyle. No one seemed to have the answer, but even without anybody's help, I was gradually withdrawing from my old ways, my old friends, and my old habits.

From some source I couldn't identify, I seemed to be gaining a new perspective on the gay life and the self-serving nature of its relationships. As I tried to make changes, I encountered either fiery rage or icy dismissal from people I'd known for years.

A man from my Drummers group invited me to his house for dinner one night. He wanted me to watch some new gay porn video he had bought. I told him I wasn't interested, and he became infuriated with me. "What's your problem, John?" he challenged, all but spitting the words out. "Are you too righteous for your friends?"

"It's not that, Carl," I insisted. "I'm just trying to do things a little differently—"

"John, let me tell you something," he interrupted angrily. "You're full of ..."

Despite such reactions, I wrote to 50 gay friends. In my letters, I let them know I had decided to leave the gay social world. I thought they were my close friends, but to my astonishment, not one wrote back. I never saw most of them again.

I talked to Ben, and at least he seemed to take me seriously. But he felt estranged from me, and though he still treasured my friendship, he didn't know how to deal with my newfound faith. He was really my only remaining homosexual friend, and the sudden, unexpected, and complete loss of my social world thrust me into a kind of solitude and isolation I'd never known before.

As I grew in my understanding of spiritual truth, my eyes opened and I could see that my gay friendships had been more shallow than I'd ever realized, and that the homosexual way of life was extremely dangerous emotionally. My growing awareness gave me a strange feeling—as if I were an explorer leaving one country without knowing anything about the one I would discover next.

During those early months of my renewed faith, I read the Bible continually. I got acquainted with Jesus by studying the book of Matthew, and my love and respect for Him increased with every passage and every conversation He had with the sinners He encountered. The story of His death and resurrection convinced me of His love, and Tom and Denise helped me understand that nothing I could do would ever make Him love me less.

It's hard to describe the impact Jesus' love had on me. I had been searching for love my entire life. Now, for the first time, I actually felt that I was completely loved and accepted. That alone was changing me deep inside, and without my even understanding it, my entire perspective on life was being transformed.

One day I phoned my mother and said, "Mom, you're not going to believe this. Do you remember how I joined that Christian youth group when I was 15? Well, I've been trying to get to know God again. And you know what? I don't think I have to be gay anymore. Maybe I wasn't really born gay after all."

Mom caught her breath. "I can't believe it!" she said. "I know you haven't really been happy, John, so I was asking God to help you. I prayed, 'God, if You're out there and if there's some way You could help John not be gay anymore, would You do it?'"

"You're kidding!" I replied, amazed that she would be praying about anything, let alone that.

What could we say? We were both astonished and excited. And above all else, we were hopeful. Something really was happening inside me. Even my sexual desires seemed to have diminished. God was at work, and I couldn't begin to imagine what He was going to do next.

Though Jesus was very real to me, I ached with a deep lone-liness that seemed to increase with every passing day. Some-times I'd reach for the phone and then shake my head sadly, realizing I had no close friends left to call. I'd sit at home fight-ing tears because I had no one to go out with and no place to go alone. I couldn't help but wonder what God was doing in my life. At that point, I wasn't entirely convinced He was doing the right thing!

Temptation continued to haunt me after I rededicated my life to Christ. I was feeling a great deal of stress because I seemed to be caught between two worlds and didn't really belong in either. Seeing my struggle, Tom and Denise gave me a book to read. It was titled *Beyond Rejection*, and in the back it gave the name of a national group called Exodus International that helps homosexuals reclaim their heterosexuality. They operated a live-in program called Love in Action (LIA).

Feeling a surge of hope, I wrote for some information. Meanwhile, Tom and Denise stopped by LIA on a trip to North-ern California and reported back that it looked like a place where deep healing really took place in the lives of gay men and lesbian women. Once I started to receive its mailings, I began to think it might offer the chance I needed for change. I called and asked for an application.

Along with it, LIA sent materials explaining how the pro-gram's classes, counseling, and Bible studies worked to help gays identify and deal with the underlying causes of their homosexuality. If accepted, I would live in a residence with other men trying to leave homosexuality; we'd have a house leader and his assistant to supervise us. I would need to get a full-time job in the area to support myself.

In early fall, I received word that my application had been approved. Before Christmas, I quit my job, packed my bags, lined up a new job near LIA, and caught a plane for San Fran-cisco. From there I got on a bus and headed north to San Rafael, where LIA was located.

As I left the bus, suitcases in hand, I noticed that a man in his 60s was standing nearby, watching the passengers disembark. "John? John Paulk?" he asked.

"Yes, I'm John," I answered. I extended my hand to shake his, but instead he embraced me, holding me firmly in his strong arms.

"I'm Frank Worthen from Love in Action," he told me. "Welcome home!"

Frank, who had founded LIA, drove me to New Hope House, my home for at least the next year. Nobody else was there when we arrived, so Frank showed me to my room, where the only open bed was a top bunk. After he left, I climbed up and wondered once again about the other men in the program. *What kind of strange gay men would show up at a place like this? Rejects,* I imagined, *who just couldn't make it in the gay world. Who cares,* I finally decided. *The less attractive they are, the better for me.*

Soon I fell asleep. When I awoke, the other residents had returned. Since it was New Year's Eve, we had LIA's traditional worship service, praying in the new year and asking God to help us all complete the program and leave the gay lifestyle.

I looked forward to most of the program. What I dreaded was the idea of going to church; because of my experience with people like those protesters at the gay pride parade, I loved God but hated Christians. After my recommitment to Christ, Tom and Denise had "done church" for me, sparing me from having to darken a sanctuary door. Yet LIA required us to attend the nearby Church of the Open Door. Frank assured us that the people there were loving and accepting, but I remained skeptical—and terrified.

That first Sunday, however, Pastor Mike Riley introduced the new group from LIA, told the congregation why we were there, and asked the people to pray for us. They responded with loud applause, and many came over to greet us warmly after the service. I was pleasantly shocked, and I've loved that church ever since.

Anne

⌐∞⌐

During those early months of my involvement with Exodus, I started making positive changes.

One particular night, I saw a video about mothers made by Starla Allen of Desert Stream Ministry, another Exodus outreach located in Southern California. Starla pointed out that some aspects of lesbianism involve the rejection of our mothers as role models. The more she talked, the more her message struck me deep in my heart.

I began to recall times in high school when I'd thought that only a supermom was an adequate mom. I had always respected women who worked professionally, were sophisticated, and had a wall full of diplomas. In contrast, my own mom had grown up in the Depression and hadn't even graduated from high school. It was an understatement to say I didn't appreciate her for who she was. Consequently, I had long rejected her as my role model.

The video brought all that to mind. Afterward, Anita Worthen—Frank Worthen's wife and the leader of the Friday-night women's meetings I attended—asked, "Does anybody want prayer?" There were only three of us present. Nobody spoke. Finally I said, "If no one else is going to say anything, you can pray for me."

Anita placed me in the middle of the group, and the other women laid their hands on me and began to pray. After a few minutes, Anita said, "Anne, I think you need to forgive your mother."

Her comment started a tug-of-war in my mind. I didn't think I held any particular anger toward my mother, but I didn't want to be like her, either, and didn't respect the kind of woman she was. Still, these didn't seem like the kind of ugly feelings I'd need to repent of. After wrestling with these thoughts for a few moments, I gave in. I said, "I want to forgive my mom. I want You to know, God, that I will accept her for who she is and will start to appreciate the things that are beautiful about her instead of continually complaining about the things I don't like."

I didn't feel any emotion at all. But the next day, Mom asked if I wanted to go shopping—I was still living with my parents then—and I said, "Sure, let's spend some time together." I could hardly believe the words had come out of my mouth.

I can't tell you why, but for the first time in my life I enjoyed shopping. It was amazing, because I was with my mother for three full hours. I led the whole shopping experience. I actually found three dresses that I wanted to purchase, and she bought them for me. I had never been motivated to wear a dress since I was four years old. Up until that shopping spree, if anybody had tried to make me wear a dress, I'd have rejected the idea with vehemence. Now, after a simple prayer, within 48 hours, I'd had a major emotional change.

It was strange to me at the time, but now I understand it a lot better. By deciding to "forgive" my mother for simply being who she was, I began to see her in a more positive light. And over time, I also started to move away from rejecting her and being critical toward her.

In April 1988, I visited the women at the Love in Action live-in program and spent the weekend to see if I was interested in moving in the following year. It was quite an adventure. A couple of the women nearly had a fist fight while I was there, arguing about the clothes dryer. I found myself on my knees in the living room, praying that they wouldn't box each other's lights out. It felt, at the time, as if that was exactly where they were headed.

One was a large Texan who had disrupted my friend Renee's life by taking her clothes out of the dryer while they were still wet. The dryer had stopped, but instead of turning it on again and drying Renee's clothes the rest of the way, the Texan had self-centeredly taken them out and left them in a damp, wrinkly pile. Renee made her displeasure known clearly and loudly. While all this was going on, another roommate was in the kitchen—cooking, humming a little tune, and ignoring the whole thing.

I rushed into the kitchen and said, "Megan! What are you doing? Why aren't you upset? Why don't you stop them?"

She shrugged and answered, "Oh, I don't care, let 'em have at it."

The house leaders weren't there at the time, but once they heard about the incident, they imposed a serious penalty: no more washer and dryer in the apartment. Their explanation was uncomplicated: "Okay, you've lost your privileges. All of you."

Those women never actually came to blows, but they came close. I think they stopped because I was on my knees, praying. They came in, saw me, and practically burst out laughing.

Even in the midst of an incident like that, I saw that the women in the program were changing. It was as if God said, "Anne, there's something incredibly valuable going on here. You've seen the ugly stuff, but you know there are other things going on—beautiful things that you can't always see."

Everybody, including Renee, kept saying, "I can't believe you're still interested in coming to this ministry!" But I felt God leading me, and it was real life. These women weren't putting on airs or being programmed to respond in certain ways. They were working through issues together. And that made a big impression on me.

I decided to join the live-in program the next year. But before I moved in, I prayed, *Lord, I really want to discuss what's going on with my parents. I want to let them know what my struggle has been, to be open about it.* But I was shivering in my boots just thinking about it. It was especially difficult since they had never wanted to know hard truths.

Lord, I prayed, *please help me. I want to be honest with my parents, but it would be really helpful if You'd have them ask me if I'm homosexual.*

Not a week later, my mother asked, seemingly out of the blue, "Anne, are you gay?"

That was very out of character for her, an amazing answer to prayer. "Well, Mom," I replied, "I've had those feelings for most of my life. But I don't want to be that way anymore. I'm a Christian now, and I want to overcome those feelings."

We sat and talked in the family room for quite a while. Then my dad came in and I told him, too. We discussed the situation, and both my parents said, "We don't want to make you feel you have to change. We want you to know that we will accept you whether you change and leave homosexuality or not."

That conversation was wonderful! It gave me the freedom to make any decision I felt necessary. More importantly, it demonstrated the unconditional love for which I'd always longed.

That September, I went to a Michael Card concert. Sometime during the program, he said, "You know, we pray a lot and ask God for a lot of things. But we also need to say, 'What do You want me to do? Share Your heart with me, God.' Let's do that right now."

Michael prayed, and the whole auditorium was absolutely silent. Suddenly, in my mind I heard words that could not have come from me: *I will heal you, Anne. I want to heal you.*

I thought, *Gosh, that doesn't sound like my voice. What is this?* That was the first time I'd ever heard God speak to me directly. I walked out of there no longer wondering if someone can really leave homosexuality. I now had the assurance that God was going to do it in me.

With several other women who were struggling like me, I entered the LIA live-in program on December 30, 1988. As I got to know the other women, I saw that each of us brought her own unique history, her own load of baggage, and we couldn't leave it outside the door. We had all come for healing. And we were all welcome at Love in Action.

In January 1989, all of us involved with LIA planned an outing to San Francisco's Pier 39, a shopping district near the Golden Gate Bridge. I had lived in the Bay Area for 14 years, so I knew exactly where I wanted to go. Well in advance of the event, I asked a women's leader if I could take my friends to some particular shops.

"Well, if there are three of you together, you can go," she promised.

We had an accountability system in place to protect and preserve each woman's desire for change. I had already told some of my friends that I would show them the more interesting shops along the way. And I definitely wanted to get myself to the chocolate shop at the end of the pier—that was my main goal. In all honesty, it was just about my only goal.

Once we got there, however, I noticed that the woman I'd asked for permission wasn't with us. Instead, the male leaders had taken charge of the event, and no one had told them I was cleared to take my friends down to the end of the pier.

I soon learned that someone named John Paulk was organizing this event. He split us up into groups of about eight. We all took off in the same direction, and at the pace we were going, I knew it was unlikely that we would ever get where I wanted to go. So I asked John, "Could I take these two girls and go down to the chocolate shop?"

John shook his head and told me, "No."

I was persistent. "I already asked Joan," I explained, "and she said it was all right."

John interpreted that as a rebellious response from me and decided on the spot that I couldn't submit to his leadership. I, on the other hand, felt that he was totally unreasonable as well as bossy.

John thought I was bossy, too, and we didn't hit it off at all. In fact, we pushed every negative button either one of us had. That event in San Francisco was our first "big" interaction, and neither of us was the least bit impressed with the other.

John
～∞～

Immediately after I joined LIA at the start of 1988, my fears about the quality of the gay men there vanished into thin air as my eyes started following Brad wherever he went. He was handsome and blond, and he reminded me painfully of Matt. As quickly as possible, I got to know him and grew more and more intensely attracted to him. My desire for change was quickly eclipsed by my desire for Brad. But I hid it as well as possible and continued with the program, desperately hoping that somewhere along the way, the two of us might end up together.

Oh, but it felt good to be in love again!

The first Sunday at Church of the Open Door, I was glad when my gaze landed on Brad. Our eyes met and we smiled at each other, a happy twinkle in our eyes.

Brad and I toyed with our attraction for several weeks. We secretly held hands, wrote each other notes, and even managed to share some exploratory caresses. We very nearly found ourselves sexually entangled.

Our secret turned out not to be so secret after all, however, because at that point a couple of the leaders intervened and stopped us. I found myself pouring out a tearful confession to my house leader, whose name was John Smid. "I never imagined that I would be attracted to somebody here!" I exclaimed.

"Why should you be surprised, John?" he gently responded. "This program is here to help you learn about your attractions—where they come from and what you should do about them."

I wasn't happy with the restrictions that were placed on Brad and me. I was even less thrilled when he suddenly became infatuated with someone else. But in the midst of my jealousy and disappointment, I came to a clear and indisputable realization: *I don't want to live this way anymore.*

I'd had enough of the wild, excruciating emotions that inevitably accompanied homosexual attractions. I wanted to be whole, healthy, and free. So my little fling with Brad had actually turned out to be a good thing, because it had shown me, once and for all, the real nature of the gay life—a life I wanted to leave behind forever.

Anne   Early on in the Love in Action program, I found
myself feeling drawn to a woman in my house. At
first I was disturbed and felt guilty, but before
long the situation turned out to be an ideal opportunity for me
to begin working through all the elements of an attraction.

I went to my house leaders and said, "Look, this is where
I'm at. I feel attracted to Karen."

The leaders weren't offended but instead began to work
with me, helping me understand some basic principles about
dealing with it. They weren't surprised—it was a common
occurrence with new residents—and they were glad to take
advantage of any learning opportunity that came along.

The more I examined the various factors and feelings
involved in my infatuation, the less I was attracted to the
woman. I knew I needed to see Karen as she was—nothing
more, nothing less. And as I became aware of all her peculiari-
ties, problems, and paranoia—and the way she artfully manip-
ulated people—the whole attraction quickly diminished.

Our leaders helped us all work through our feelings by asking us to list the women we'd been attracted to and to consider
why we'd been drawn to them. We'd say things like "Oh, her
eyes were beautiful" or "her hair was so sensuous," describing
physical, outward things. But as we learned, regardless of the
physical attributes we had admired, as lesbians we were
always drawn to a sort of distorted mirror—an idealized image
of ourselves.

As I went through my own list, I found that was all too true
of me. I had been drawn to qualities I wanted for myself. I
learned from the others at LIA that if you're involved in a lesbian relationship, you're trying to absorb your partner's qualities by having an intimate relationship with her. And that's not
love at all.

By now I was convinced that God's love is real love, the love
I truly wanted. With every passing day, I was more determined
to get beyond my past and experience it.

John The year 1989 found me hard at work in the LIA program. We spent hours in Bible study and prayer, as well as in exploring our homosexual urges, identifying their root causes, and consciously retraining our responses. We learned about the parenting dynamics that had played such a key role in all our lives. We talked about pornography and molestation. We discussed peer influences. We reflected upon the people we had attached ourselves to in the past and tried to understand the nature of our attractions.

As the months passed, I started to see changes in myself, subtle changes that might not have caught my attention except that they were so new, so unlike the old me. One day, I decided to respond to a gay salesman as if I were straight. In the past, I would have played into his personality. But this time, I took a different approach; I did everything I could think of to act straight.

On another occasion, as I stepped into an elevator with another man, I noticed that he was checking me out, giving me not-so-subtle signals that said, "I'm gay and available. Are you interested?" In the past I would have been flattered, but now I felt indignation. So I sent a signal of my own—I switched my ring from my right hand to the left to give the impression I was married, crossed my arms, and turned toward him so that the ring would be unmistakable. My message was clear: "Not me, buddy. You're wasting your time."

As I reflected on these and other similar incidents, it occurred to me that something was shifting at the core of my being. God was doing what I couldn't accomplish on my own— I no longer wanted to be identified as a gay man.

My outgoing personality led to wonderful opportunities to speak to various groups about our program and the efforts we were making. LIA sponsored evening rallies in which men in the program would visit churches around the San Francisco area, introducing them to our ministry and telling them about the changes taking place in our lives.

An amazing surprise also took place that year, and it

changed me and my family forever. A few of us from LIA had traveled to Eugene, Oregon, to tell churches there about our ministry. I was really looking forward to the evening because my sister, Vicky, was going to attend. By then she had graduated from Georgetown University, and she was living in Portland. She had strongly disapproved of my decision to live at LIA, and I wanted her to hear what we had to say.

"Can you drive down from Portland to hear me sing?" I had asked her.

"I'll be there," she had promised.

Sure enough, she was there. The song I sang, "Can You Reach My Friend?" describes reaching out to a person who doesn't know God yet.

After the service, I saw that Vicky was crying but didn't know why. Anita Worthen, who was standing with me, said, "I see God is working on your sister. Why don't you ask to pray with her?"

"No," I said, "no one in *my* family would want to become a Christian." But Vicky was obviously distraught, so I went over to her and put my arm around her.

"You looked like an angel as you sang," she said through her tears. "You're so different."

I suddenly felt emboldened to tell her about God's love and how He was changing me and filling me with joy. Then I asked, "Do you want to pray the sinner's prayer and become a Christian too?"

"Yes," she said, and so I had the thrill of helping my sister place her trust in Jesus Christ and know with certainty that her sins, like mine, were fully forgiven by a gracious God. I also had the pleasure of being reassured that if Vicky saw major changes taking place in me, I was indeed moving out of homosexuality.

Anne

      ∞

In June 1989, along with five other women in the program, I attended an Exodus conference in San Antonio, Texas. What an incredible experience it was! One of the first things we noticed was how far we'd come in six short months. All of us could see that some of the other new attendees, involved with weekly support groups elsewhere, hadn't delved nearly as far into their issues. For all the trouble we'd been through, it had been worth it. Through all the arguing and all the struggling, we were actually learning, and learning quickly. That was good news.

Many of the women attending the national conference were obviously still caught up in infatuations with other women's looks. Thankfully, in our group, we were focused on seeing past "attractive" outer façades of the women we met. We were committed to doing less idolizing and more building of real, long-term, straight friendships.

After returning home from the conference, I received a letter from a young woman named Joy that crystallized the importance of our efforts. Joy had been attending a weekly group in the Great Lakes area. She had been immediately attracted to me in San Antonio.

"Dear Anne," she wrote, "I really enjoyed getting to know you. I just wanted you to know that if there is anything I can do for you, just let me know. I mean, if you ever get sick and need to have someone take care of you, just call and I'll fly out ..."

I wrote back to her, "Joy, I really appreciate your kind offer, but I barely know you, and it takes a great deal of time to build a friendship of that caliber. I did enjoy your company also. But I receive a great deal of support, in those practical ways, from friends God has placed around me here."

That exchange came as a sweet reward, enabling me to see my progress. At long last, I was learning that really good friendships are built over time, slowly and nonobsessively, and that healthy relationships grow through misunderstandings, disappointment, and forgiveness. I had discovered enough to know that Joy's attention was probably fleeting. She had been drawn to some image of me that had materialized in her imagination. She had no idea who I really was, faults and all.

One night while at the conference, I was late for a worship session. There were at least 500 people there, and when I walked in, I couldn't find any of the women from our program. One of the program men saw me, however, and motioned for me to join his group. They made room for me and I sat in the midst of them, worshiping and listening to the teaching.

Later that night I had to walk across the campus alone. Glancing over my shoulder, I realized a man was walking about 50 steps behind me. Suddenly I was so afraid—the old terror overwhelmed me. I had long feared that a man was going to rape me. Intellectually, I knew it was just a lingering fear from my childhood. But emotionally, I was nearly overwhelmed by panic. My heart pounded faster and faster as I monitored the man's progress.

But that night I caught myself and decided it was time to face my fear. So I stopped, waited, and intended to let him pass me. But instead of being some anonymous assailant or even just a stranger, the man turned out to be one of the Exodus ministry leaders, Bob Brown from Seattle.

"Oh, hi, Anne!" Bob greeted me, never imagining that I had been afraid. Then he went on to say something extraordinary: "You know, when I saw you worshiping tonight with the men, I had this picture of you being protected. There you were, this precious woman, and you had the protection of all those men around you."

It had never occurred to me before that any man—or men—could protect me. Now the thought ran through my head, *What? Is that supposed to mean that some men can be trusted?* The more I thought about it, the more I realized that protectiveness is a role a man should take toward a woman. It's a godly response. Bob had introduced that new thought into my mind, and God had led him to do so in the midst of my fear.

Bob went his way, and I went mine. But for the rest of the evening, I continued to reflect on that new idea. Once I had thought it through, I found that it had introduced still another new thought to me: Perhaps at some point a man might enter my life in a significant way, and maybe it wouldn't be all that bad. Maybe a man's company wasn't something to fear. These, for me, were revolutionary thoughts because, for the first time, they introduced the possibility of matrimony. Until then, I had been mortally afraid of marriage.

Through circumstances that took place in our residence, the Lord also worked another aspect of my healing. I came to realize that I had to forgive my father for being so critical of me. I had long resented his habit of being quick to point out my faults without first pointing out my strengths. I think he just assumed that I knew he loved me, so he never mentioned it. That was true in his relationships with all his children. But I still held a lot of anger toward him, and it was time to let it go.

By now I was changing quickly on the inside. Changes were taking place in my outward appearance, too. From time to time, women from the church came to our residence to help us with our grooming, posture, and overall appearance. One of them taught us which colors we should wear, and another helped us learn to apply makeup. Some women in the program were more receptive to these sessions than others. My friend Donna recoiled from the whole makeup thing and nearly washed the skin off her face trying to get rid of it. The rest of us cooperated, but in varying degrees. All of this was fun; it was new. We didn't have to adopt any part of it if we didn't want to. But we got a chance to see what it was like to be a "normal" woman.

It was my habit to jog around an area where there were dense bushes. And despite facing my fear that one night with Bob Brown, I was still concerned that a man might jump out of the bushes and assault me sexually. At that point, I would have been more willing to die than to be raped.

As I jogged, my eyes cautiously scanned each bush, and I braced myself, poised and ready to fight off any attacker. This carried over to the times when I wasn't jogging, but I wasn't aware of how it had become part of my normal body posture. I had learned to look tough; I carried myself with my elbows out, my shoulders square, and a hard expression on my face. My look was both masculine and self-protective.

One day as I jogged, I recalled what I had been learning from the Psalms: The Lord is my strong tower, He is my rock, He is my protector, He is my fortress. It then dawned on me that I was being my own fortress. I was being my own protector, and I had never noticed it before. What a powerful revelation that was, and yet it made me feel very vulnerable.

I talked the idea over with the Lord. *But God, shouldn't I be looking out for myself?* I asked. *You don't want me defenseless again, do You? Are You sure You're going to be there for me?*

As I read the Bible night after night, each passage seemed to reinforce the same idea: "'Not by might nor by power, but by my Spirit' says the LORD Almighty" (Zechariah 4:6). I talked this over with Annie, one of my friends. "Do you think it's dangerous to just trust God to protect me?" I asked. "I mean, when I'm jogging, I'm really afraid somebody is going to grab me or attack me or something."

Annie nodded and replied, "Yeah, I know. I've got some fears like that, too. But I think God wants us to entrust ourselves to Him so He can take care of us. After all, He says He'll never leave us or forsake us."

"Yeah, I know. But it's just so scary."

"It's scary for me, too," Annie admitted. "But I think we can count on God's promises that He'll be our protector—He sure made enough of them in the Psalms. And if He's our protector, that means we can relax and enjoy ourselves."

After discussing my fears with several more friends, I decided to take God at His Word and let Him back it up, even if I was doing so with "fear and trembling." I made up my mind that in the future, I would approach jogging with a different attitude. I wouldn't go out at midnight or be careless, but I would not be overly concerned either. I would redirect my mind and not look behind every bush. *God*, I prayed, *I'm going to believe*

that You are my protector. And I'm going to act as if I believe it.
Because of that commitment on my part, He began to transform
me from within, making me feel protected and loved. That, in
turn, made me feel more like a woman.

My new sense of security affected my posture. The truth
was, all of us in the program realized we didn't carry ourselves
very well. One of the house leaders had remarked, not too
kindly, "You all walk like men." I can still see three of us awk-
wardly trying to walk in a more feminine way and evaluating
one another's progress. We tried to analyze the difference
between the way we walked and the way other women walked,
and then we began to rehearse. It was kind of an adolescent
experience, like learning to dance.

In order to improve my appearance, I decided to buy my
first pair of heels, to wear to my new job at AAA Insurance. I
took one of the guys from the men's program shopping with
me, assuming he'd have more fashion sense than I did. In fact, I
suspect that he knew more about fashion than all us program
women put together.

"I really want to get a pair of low pumps," I explained to
him, "maybe black patent leather."

Together we picked out these one-inch pumps that fit perfectly. When I wore them to church the first time, everybody
noticed. All the ex-gay guys came up and exclaimed, "Oh, Anne,
you look so great!" Unfortunately, I felt humiliated because, the
way I heard it, they were pointing out how bad I'd looked before.
I was ashamed that the contrast in my appearance was so obvious.

John Paulk was the fifth person who approached me, and he
said, "Oh Anne, those shoes look really nice on you!"

I'd heard enough compliments by then. "Leave me alone!" I
barked at him. "Don't compliment me. I just want to be left
alone."

John walked off, muttering, "I'll never compliment that
woman again as long as I live!"

I can't say I blamed him.

John   As the men in the LIA program talked about
being estranged from their fathers and the role
that had played in developing their homosexuality, I wondered if I had correctly understood my own dad.
Finally one day, I got out all the letters he had ever sent me,
arranged them in chronological order, and read them slowly.
Over and over I saw Dad saying, "I love you. Can I do anything
for you?" and so on.

When I finished the last letter, I realized in a flash of insight,
My dad does love me! I hadn't been able to receive it before, to
accept it, because he hadn't expressed love in the verbal, effusive way I wanted. But now I saw that Dad did love me in his
own way, and that was good enough.

I called Dad, told him what I had done, and said I was sorry
for not believing him when he'd said he loved me. Then I asked
for his forgiveness.

"John," he responded, "I do love you, and I don't think there's
anything to forgive. But if you need to hear it, I forgive you."

That proved to be a significant moving-forward point for me.
Afterward, I could tell other guys, "Receive the love your father
is able to give, and let God and other Christians fill in the gaps."

My dad still doesn't express love as enthusiastically as I'd
like, by the way; he is who he is. But God enabled me to look at
him as someone needing to be forgiven for his failures just as
God forgave me.

That same year, having reconciled with Dad, I also found
that it was time to deal with another "person" in my life. I was
still dragging Candi around like a ball and chain. I constantly
referred to her and to how good I had been in drag. Then one
day, a housemate named Jerry asked, "John, we don't know you
that way—when are you going to let Candi go?"

Stunned momentarily, I realized he was right. So I started
asking God to help me put Candi in the past and stop thinking
about and referring to her. *God help me,* I prayed. *You know my
heart's desire is to see myself as a heterosexual man and to be respected*

as a man. Help me to cut all spiritual and emotional ties to Candi. I can't do it without you.

And in the days and weeks that followed, He made that change in me as well.

Anne In early 1990, one of the Love in Action women's house leaders—one who didn't like me very much—moved out. Only four of us remained in the home. We decided to stay there and live as roommates the second year with minimal structure, getting together just one night a week to talk and keep some kind of accountability between us.

The remaining house leader, who'd always had a sympathetic heart toward me, stayed with us. Before long, I began to feel attracted to her, sexualizing the kindness she had shown me. Over several weeks, my attraction to her fluctuated—increasing one day, then diminishing the next. Anyone watching could have seen that it followed my old pattern of infatuation. But no one was watching—no one but God.

One night I was at a prayer time with my friend Renee and some others. We were praying for someone else, but Renee felt led to tell me, "Anne, some really difficult times are coming up for you, and I'm not sure how you're going to make it through. I just want to warn you that God has given me this information so you can be prepared. He's going to test you, and it's going to be real difficult."

I knew exactly what that message meant. I was already aware that my desires were getting the best of me. The LIA residents would be moving toward the end of the year, and I was insecure about where I was going to live. I longed to live with the house leader, but I wasn't sure if that would work out. I wasn't even sure it should work out.

It seemed to me that she was slightly attracted to me, too. She left doors open in an emotional sense. Meanwhile, my roommates were finding other places to live, and I was feeling more and more insecure. I told the Lord, *Here's what I'd like to do,* and I listed a series of locations and ideas. I concluded by saying, *Please direct me.* But I was beginning to feel that I would be homeless. And the more insecure I got, the more my infatuation with this woman increased.

God sometimes waits till the last minute to act. He'll wait until everybody else has moved and you have a week to go, and then He'll provide a way. That's what He was doing with me. And during all this stress, I leaned heavily upon my house leader for emotional support, knowing that the time was coming when I probably wouldn't be living with her anymore.

One night we all went out to dinner and had a great time, laughing and talking. When we returned to the house, we were kind of sad, knowing we were about to leave one another for good. I couldn't resist going to this woman's room to say good-bye.

"Gosh, I'm really going to be sad," I told her as I entered. "I'm going to miss our being around each other."

I was fully aware of my feelings for her. I sensed a similar response from her—a kind of sexual energy that almost crackled in the air. Even though she was across the room, we both felt vibrant with excitement. As we moved closer to each other, our feelings grew. We were facing an old, familiar temptation, and we weren't facing it well.

As I hugged her, I realized, *Oh my, things could go quickly downhill from here. I know what happens next.* God knew what would happen, too, and He prompted Wendy, another woman in the house, to check up on us at that moment.

Wendy woke up three times with the thought that she should go to the house leader's room. But each time she dismissed the thought, saying, "God, what are You doing? Is this really You? I'm sleepy." Finally, Wendy reluctantly got out of her bed, walked down the hall, and came into the room where I was hugging the other woman, about to kiss her and get into real trouble.

Wendy just stood there, speechless, for a minute. Then she announced, "God told me to get up and check on you guys." And that was the end of the temptation.

I was brokenhearted about what had happened. I had learned so much, come so far, only to fail miserably and end up (so it seemed) right back where I'd started. Again and again I cried out, *God, how could I do that?* I confessed tearfully, *I thought I was doing so well, and look where I am. I have absolutely no self-control. I would have had sex with her.*

While God eventually answered my prayer by providing ideal living circumstances—a quiet place where I could garden and have my cat—I continued to grieve for at least two months, weighed down with regret. *Lord, this sin is still so deep in my heart,* I told Him again and again. *I haven't changed at all! What are You going to do with me?*

John   "Anita and I have been directing Love in Action here in San Rafael for 17 years, and we've decided to move to the Philippines and begin a similar ministry in Manila." That was Frank Worthen's stunning announcement to all of us in the LIA program, and it took our breath away. Then he asked me privately afterward, "John, would you be willing to take Anita's place as administrator here? Would you pray about it?"

Frank's confidence in me was a huge confirmation of all God was doing in my life. To my amazement, he saw me as a new man bearing no resemblance to the drag queen I'd been in my homosexual past. My vision for complete healing was becoming a reality, and it was happening more quickly than I'd ever imagined possible.

The impact of my new life even began to make ripples across the country, reaching people I'd known in my old life. Ben was the one gay friend I'd kept during my recovery process, and the subject of God's work in my life had come up in our conversations more than once. I was shocked when he confided that the new John Paulk saddened him. He admitted that his life wasn't going anywhere. "I can see that you're involved in something really worthwhile," he acknowledged. "You seem so peaceful, and it couldn't be more obvious that you're changing—not just on the outside but also on the inside. Is it spiritual? What is it?"

I explained that Jesus Christ was at work in my heart, making me a new person from the inside out. And before the conversation ended, to my great joy, he told me he wanted the same thing to happen in his life. I prayed with Ben, and he believed in Jesus as his Savior and Lord. With hope surging in me, I suggested, "Who knows—someday you may decide to join the Love in Action program." He promised to give the idea some thought once he had finished college.

During my time at LIA, I felt no pressure from others to begin dating women. In fact, the thought of it was so foreign—and frightening—that I didn't take seriously the possibility that I might become romantically involved with a woman someday.

But I soon began realizing that my desires to only be with men were changing. When I was with them, I just didn't feel the same challenge and interest that I once had. I was comfortable being male, and I wanted what was different. When I was in the gay lifestyle, I had enjoyed talking with women about the most intimate details of their lives. But now I felt the natural male/female barrier and didn't want to hear those kinds of things. God had helped me remain sexually abstinent for over four years, and now He was preparing me to take the next step in my healing.

In Bible study one afternoon, my eyes were drawn to a woman named Melanie. Sunlight through the window highlighted her blonde hair, making it look soft and shimmering. Her beauty was captivating, and I couldn't seem to take my eyes off her.

This was an entirely new experience for me. Her femininity

was very different from the masculine qualities I had always craved in my male partners. The more I thought about it, the more I was convinced that I was ready to start dating women. The idea was scary, but its time had come.

"Everything He
Has Said,
He Will
Do..."

Anne   Despite my close call with the house leader and
  ◌≫◌   the terrible grief I felt, my heart continued to be
changed, even beyond my own comprehension.
One day a young couple came into our AAA office to apply for
insurance. They appeared to be married. The young man wore
a skin-tight shirt and was very muscular. The two of them were
hanging all over each other, and as I watched them I thought,
Oh, they're young lovers. How sweet. Then the man turned around,
and I realized it was a woman. My response was unlike any I'd
ever had before—I was repulsed, and I felt saddened by the
scene.

A lesbian relationship had been my fantasy since I was
seven or eight years old. I knew my role perfectly—I would
have been the woman who looked like a man. And now, to my
surprise, I recoiled at the sight of it.

Days later, I was invited to a women's softball tournament.
As I sat in the bleachers and watched the women moving
around the dugout and taking their places on the field—women
I knew to be lesbians—I wasn't the least bit attracted to them.
Instead, I felt sorrowful about their self-protectiveness. They
were covering all their vulnerability with outward displays of
masculinity, and if their needs were being met at all, they were
being met in an inadequate way. My heart broke for these
women, and I was taken off guard by my reaction.

After those two incidents, I knew that God had changed my
orientation deep within. I was no longer a lesbian. And I understood that this final and ultimate change had come out of my
grief and mourning. During a prayer time with my regular Bible
study group, one of the pastors prayed for me and felt led by the

Lord to say, "God is going to do a new thing for you, Anne—
something that's going to be so exciting and wonderful, you'll
hardly believe it when it happens."

Not long after that, I attended a marriage rededication; a
man who had been homosexual was rededicating himself to his
wife and his marriage. As I sat in the audience, John Paulk got
up and sang, "My Redeemer is faithful and true, everything He
has said, He will do...." I was stunned by the incredibly beautiful song lyric, and as I watched John while he sang, I was moved
to tears. I was suddenly aware of the purity of his heart and of
his openness toward God.

I saw something in him that I admired and treasured. Then,
out of nowhere, my heart began to flutter. My hands became
sweaty. I sat there asking myself, *What on earth is going on with
me?* Never before had I experienced those feelings toward a man.

As a house leader, John had learned to respond to leadership authority. I had been watching from a distance and knew
how God had been molding him. He was no longer bossy, controlling, or difficult to deal with. Whenever I was around John, I
couldn't help but notice that he had become gentler with others.
One day after church, I watched as he sat down and put his arm
around Madeleine, a mother whose teenage son had recently
entered homosexuality.

"John, I feel like such a failure!" she sobbed. "I don't know
what to do."

"You don't need to blame yourself," he said comfortingly.
"Your son is an adult, and he's making adult choices. We just
need to pray for him."

"I know, but it's just so terrible!" she wailed. "What if he
gets AIDS? And what will his father say?" She was shaking with
emotion.

John's voice remained calm, soft, and reassuring. "You
know, Madeleine, God is able to bring Rich through this and
back to Himself," he told her. "He did it for me, and He can do
it for Rich. Do you want me to pray with you?"

As Madeleine wept, John kept his arm firmly around her shoulders. He began to pray, "Lord, we come to You seeking Your help for Madeleine's son Richard. Her heart is broken by the news that he's involved in homosexuality. Please reach him and help him to find You in the midst of his struggle. Lead him away from temptations, and draw Him to You. Help him to see how much You love him, Lord. And bring Christians into his life to help him find his way."

Not only was John a help to people in pain, but he had also matured in his leadership role. Whereas in the past he had sometimes been independent and impulsive, now he often sought input from others before making decisions. Yes, I was beginning to greatly admire this man.

Still, the likelihood of my having a relationship with him seemed absurd. So I surrendered my feelings to God and left it at that. I prayed, *Lord, look, I'm not going to go running after this guy. If these feelings are from You, You're going to have to make it work. I'm not going to do a thing.*

Soon thereafter, before his work at the LIA office began, John got a temporary job in a building near where I worked at AAA. He didn't have a car, and he asked if I could give him a ride. As we drove to work and back day after day, we found we had a lot in common. We enjoyed each other's company. I looked forward to our time together, and a friendship began.

One day I said, "Hey, maybe we should do something together sometime. Would you ever want to go to a movie or something?" That was a big step in a new direction for me.

John   My response to Anne's question was, "Yeah, maybe sometime," but later I asked myself, *Would I want to go to a movie with Anne?* At first I rejected the idea. Then I had second thoughts. *I really do enjoy Anne's company,* I decided. *Maybe someday. We'll see what happens.*

In the meantime, I started asking other women to do things

with me, simple things like walking around Sausalito or hiking across the Golden Gate Bridge. But I remained intrigued by Anne's desire to do something together and was steadily reevaluating our relationship. I admired her qualities as a woman and had noticed the changes in her over time. Though I no longer rode with her since I was now part of the LIA staff, I found myself wanting to learn more about her and her past.

My curiosity about females was growing, and though I was attracted to Anne—more than I realized at the time—I was interested in other women, too. Molly caught my attention quickly. She was gorgeous, with sandy hair and a great sense of dramatic style.

Molly had recently become a Christian, and it didn't take me long to learn that she needed a great deal of attention and nurturing. We went out several times, and although I was attracted to her physically, we didn't have many common interests. My heart was into ministry, and she didn't share that vision. She had been used and abused by a number of men in the past, and this also took its toll on our relationship. Before long, I was fairly sure I needed to break up with Molly. But I wasn't sure when to do it, what to say, or how to approach the subject. So I did nothing.

Anne   In the past, Molly had been promiscuous, and she displayed a lot of physical affection for John. For some reason, this worried me a little. I even asked him about it, and he assured me that everything was fine. But before long, at worship team practice one day, he confessed that he just wanted to dump Molly, run away as fast as he could, and not tell her why.

"Oh, no, please don't do that!" I urged him. "Just tell her you're not interested anymore." He looked a little desperate, so I added, "Let me pray for you. Let me pray that God will give you the courage to go talk to her."

John We moved out to the foyer, where people were milling around. Anne took me off to the side, and we found a place to sit. We bowed our heads and she prayed, "Lord, I ask that You would give John the words to say to Molly. Instruct him to be gentle. And Lord, I pray that You would show him who the right woman is for him."

As soon as she said that, God spoke to my heart and said, *She's right in front of you. It's Anne.*

I looked up as she continued to pray, not really hearing her anymore. I got excited and asked, *Wow, is this really You, God, telling me Anne is the right person for me?* I thought about all the things I admired about her—the gentle spirit and softness I had seen her develop over time as God healed her, the way she worked with children, the fact that she wasn't at all gossipy and never said anything bad about anybody, and the way her heart was always toward what was right.

Suddenly, I was seeing Anne in a new, more serious light.

Afterward, I did go talk with Molly, a conversation that went well as we agreed we were better off as good friends. Then she said to me, "Have you ever considered Anne Sutton? You talk about her all the time."

"Do I?" I asked in surprise. I hadn't realized I'd been doing that.

She nodded and continued, "You two seem to have so much more in common."

Unexpected as the source may have been, here was confirmation of what God had said to my spirit.

Anne One of my former roommates, Sheila, had been living in Florida, and for the past few weeks I'd been writing to her about John. After she moved back to the Bay Area, John, Sheila, and I went to San Francisco for an afternoon. We were wandering around the marina, and we ended up in a restaurant.

After we ordered, Sheila looked at John, then at me, and said, "Okay, you two, just 'fess up. John, you've been asking me about Anne. Anne, you've been writing me about John. So what's going on?"

An awkward silence fell between us. We could barely look at each other. Finally I said, "Look, Sheila, you're right. I wrote to you about these little feelings of mine ..."

I glanced over at John, both excited and terrified about what he might be thinking. "Yeah," I continued, "I'm interested in you, John. But I don't know how you feel."

"Well, I'm interested in you, too, Anne."

From that time on, we started doing things together as a couple. We were both on the worship team, so he would pick me up and take me home. We weren't "dating" yet; it felt safer for us to stay in groups while we checked each other out. But the more we got to know each other, the more I thought, *Gosh, I wouldn't date this guy if I didn't think there was a potential of getting married. And I'm starting to think there is.*

Four or five other guys had expressed an interest in me in the past year or two, and I'd gone out with some of them, but John had outshone everyone else. He was fascinating, he was different, and we were complementary in a lot of ways. He offered strength where I had weaknesses. He was unashamed to be really masculine, and he was anything but passive.

We were both well aware of the other's past. I knew he had been a drag queen. That didn't alarm me because I saw the man he had become, and it obviously wasn't the man he'd been when I first met him. He was developing into a new, respectable man of integrity. He submitted to authority. He wasn't afraid to take correction. I saw all these qualities from a distance, and they impressed me. So I allowed him to approach me more, and I let him take the lead.

One night when John and I were at rehearsal for our worship team, I really wanted him to sit by me, but I resisted the urge to ask him. I was a little disappointed when he started talking to someone else and chose a seat in a different row. But afterward, as we headed for our cars, he called out to me, "Anne, I'm going to follow you home. I just want to make sure you get there safely."

I looked at him in surprise. "That's nice of you, John," I replied. "What made you want to do that?"

"Well, sometimes I think you're a little apprehensive about being out alone at night. I want you to feel safe."

I realized, with amazement, that John had a natural desire to protect me. And I knew that feeling safe was just what I needed from a man. I also knew that if John wasn't going to be interested beyond a certain point, I could break off the relationship and that would be the end. I had developed enough self-respect not to put myself through years of dating without seeing any results.

John As Anne and I spent time together, I started to feel these strange urges coming out of nowhere to protect her, open doors for her, and walk on the outside of the sidewalk to safeguard her from traffic. I quickly took up her defense if anyone criticized her in my hearing, and I found myself becoming jealous if another man paid attention to her. Her femaleness made me feel more like a man just from our being together. Simply put, she brought out the best in me.

One day that July of 1991, Mike Riley and I were at a men's retreat, sitting on a bench overlooking the Golden Gate Bridge. The day was warm, and we were chatting. At one point I asked, "Do you think I'll ever be ready to marry and have kids of my own?"

Mike replied, "God has a wonderful way of catching you up to where you need to be, John." Then he added with conviction, "When the time comes, you'll be ready."

During lunch one day, Anne and I were eating at a fast-food restaurant near her work (though in our eyes we still weren't dating). I looked across the table at her and was struck by how dear she was becoming to me. "Anne," I said softly, "I think it's safe to say that our friendship has changed into something else—something new and different."

"What do we call it?" she asked, a puzzled look in her eyes.

I paused for a moment, trying to find the right words. "I think I'd say that you're my *girlfriend*. How does that sound?"

"Sounds good to me," she said with a laugh. "So I guess that makes you my *boyfriend*, right?"

At that moment, our surroundings seemed to fade as we stared into each other's eyes. I wanted to take her hand and hold it, but I was too nervous. *My girlfriend*, I kept saying to myself. *Anne is my girlfriend*. I could hardly believe it was true.

Anne Thanks to our untraditional experiences, John and I seemed to be struggling with more variations of fear, embarrassment, and insecurity than could possibly affect one couple. But John finally found the courage to ask me out on our first real date. The next Sunday after church, he took me to the wine country in Napa Valley—a beautiful, scenic area of rolling hills, peaceful vineyards, and elegant wineries. We toured one of the wineries together, and for the first time John took my hand in his and held it as we walked. Even in that simple gesture, we could feel a special kind of excitement between us.

John tried to appear relaxed, but I could tell he was terrified. He had been reluctant even to invite me because he wasn't sure he could "do" a date just right. It was the first time he had been in a seriously romantic situation with a girl. He was almost as nervous as I was.

At one point, John began to caress my hand gently. I had to ask him to stop—his touch was so stimulating that it almost frightened me. I had never felt a romantic response like that in all my life. I felt as though the air around us was charged with electricity. It was obvious that John and I were extremely attracted to each other in every way—spirit, soul, and body. But fear is a powerful adversary to love, and I was still afraid of investing my heart. Who could guess what would happen next?

John Our pastor, Mike Riley, had been a solid support to me throughout my process of change and growth. He'd kept an eye on me, and by now he was well aware that something was going on between Anne and me. For one thing, he'd noticed that we were always together in church. Meanwhile, the LIA grapevine was alive and well, so he soon heard various reports from others in the program that we were dating.

"I hear you and Anne Sutton are going out," he told me one day.

Still trying to find my way through the newness of the situation, I felt a little embarrassed by his question. "Yes," I said, "we've been dating."

"Since this is kind of an unusual situation for both of you, what would you think about the three of us getting together and talking things over?" he asked.

"I think it's a great idea. It's such a new experience for us," I agreed, "and, to be honest, we really don't know what we're doing!"

Mike suggested we meet at a local park and have an informal picnic. "This is an unusual situation," he said when we got together. "What does it mean to you?"

"I don't know," I answered, "But we really like it. I mean, we really like each other."

"There's something really special between us," Anne added, "and I'm not sure what to call it. But God's in it, I can tell you that."

Mike was pleased to see us together and seemed amused by our adolescent behavior. But understandably, he was concerned about our ability to navigate such uncharted waters for the first time. He asked if we would be willing to meet with him every couple of weeks and talk things over. We were both grateful for his interest and agreed with his suggestion.

Little by little, Anne and I started sharing more of ourselves with each other. One day, to my delight, she came by my office to ask my opinion of a dress she'd just bought. We often played the guitar and sang our favorite songs together. We played chess as well, and the first time was also the first time our knees touched—an unforgettable moment.

One night when she had paid me a visit, after I walked her to her car, I put my arms around her and gave her a big hug. To my surprise, I heard myself saying, "I love you, Anne." I'd never said those words to any woman outside my family.

She was speechless, and I didn't know what to do next. "You don't have to answer," I told her. "I just wanted you to know how I feel."

I took her to an Amy Grant concert for her birthday. I bought her presents. I carefully planned every date. I read every book on Christian dating that I could get my hands on. I wanted to be sure I didn't make any mistakes.

Anne, on the other hand, was feeling the effects of my determination to "do everything right." She pointed out that my intensity and assertiveness were a little overwhelming to her. "Maybe we should slow things down a little," she said.

I was devastated. My aggressive pursuit of Anne had alarmed her, and yet everything I had done, I had done from the heart. Had I damaged our relationship? Was I getting so carried away that I was losing touch with reality?

That night I got on my knees and poured my heart out to God. *Lord, Anne is so wonderful,* I prayed. *When I'm with her, I feel such joy, such sexual desire, and such a sense of my own masculinity. It's a miracle, Lord. But I really need Your help as we build a relationship. I want this to last and don't want to damage it by being overeager. Will You help me, Lord?*

I paused for a moment and quickly verbalized the thoughts that were filling my mind and heart. *And Lord,* I concluded, *if it could be Your will, would You work things out so that Anne and I can get married someday? I want her to be my wife.*

Anne John and I were always together by then, and it was so wonderful being a couple. Sometimes we'd go for walks in Mill Valley in the rain. Sometimes we'd just sit and talk. We both enjoyed doing the same kinds of things, and we were thrilled to be together. But I was still worried—were we falling in love with each other or just with the *idea* of being in love? That's when I told John I thought we should slow things down a bit.

But there was another reason as well. My responses to him were so intense that they frightened me. It didn't matter what we did; my emotional and sexual responses were overwhelming. I talked to Mike, our pastor, about it. I said, "Could you please coach John, because I don't know if he knows what he's doing to me."

Mike talked to John and he gave him a book called *Too Close, Too Soon,* which was helpful to both of us. With Mike's help, we talked about boundaries and came to an agreement about what should and shouldn't happen between us at that point. Little by little, I began to relax, and before long I was comfortable with John's expressions of affection. Weeks turned to months, and I, too, was beginning to look forward to moving into the next stages of our relationship.

One day John and I were walking through a mall, and at one of the Emporium's cosmetic counters, we met a woman John knew. Beverly was a cosmetic artist for one of the lines, an older Southern belle. She was really hilarious, with big hair, a contagious laugh, and an outgoing personality.

Beverly noticed that we were together and asked about our relationship. "Honey, has he kissed you yet?" she asked with a sly wink.

John and I had vowed that we would try to save kissing for our marriage or at least for our engagement. I don't know what I told her, but Beverly laughed and said, "Oh, c'mon honey! Let me do your makeup. He'll want to kiss you after that!"

So there I sat in the store, intimidated just by being in the cosmetic department. Fortunately, there weren't many people around since it wasn't long before closing, and she had time. It was my first experience of really having a good makeover, and Beverly did a great job. The results were remarkable, and I especially noticed that John could not take his eyes off me. He acted as if I were the most gorgeous woman in the world, constantly looking over at me with this awestruck look in his eyes.

Afterward, we drove to a restaurant called Zim's where we were going to have dessert together. While we were still in the car, all at once John, with shaky hands, placed a little ring on my pinkie finger. "I just wanted you to have this," he explained. Then he leaned over and—ignoring our vow—gave me a kiss. That first kiss was incredible! We didn't stop for a good 10 minutes. We couldn't bear to stop—it would have been impossible. So we just sat there in the car kissing, both of us on cloud nine.

Finally we went inside the restaurant, sat down at a table, and looked into each other's eyes. We could hardly speak. We held hands, but we just didn't have much to say. We managed to drink our coffee and eat our dessert, then we went dreamily back to the car. John drove me to his house, where I had parked my car. When it was time to say good-bye, we kissed and hugged again. Believe me, all systems were working!

John I decided it was time to tell Dad I had a girl-friend. I called and broke the news, saying her name was Anne and telling him a little about her. He seemed cautious, guarded, disbelieving, even skeptical. "Oh, okay ... Uh huh ... That's nice," was about all he had to say. At the same time, I sensed that he approved.

When I told Mom, she was much more excited and expressive about her joy for me.

I realized that what I was telling my parents was completely foreign. They had never before heard me say, "I've got a girlfriend." Yet at that point in my life, nothing that came out of my mouth shocked them. So they kind of went along, not sure what was happening. In their own ways, each of them tried to be as supportive as possible.

Meanwhile, Mike Riley continued to meet with Anne and me and give us counsel. One afternoon in August, as we sat at a picnic table in a park, he asked me, "So, John, assuming this relationship continues on the same path it's on now, when would you consider proposing to Anne?"

Anne and I looked at each other, startled and embarrassed that he would be so forward about something we hadn't had the courage to even begin discussing yet. But he saw that we had the makings of a really good marriage.

Groping for an answer as both Anne and Mike stared at me, I said to her, "I'll ask you by Thanksgiving."

That took her aback, and she made it clear that was too soon for her. We bantered a little about it, playing a game of cat and mouse, giggling the whole time because the entire guy-girl thing was so new and uncomfortable for us. Then she said, half in jest, "If you ever expect to marry me, you'll have to get permission from my dad first."

"You really can't expect me to ask your dad," I replied, continuing the game. "After all, I'm almost 30 years old!"

"If you ever expect to propose to me, you *will* call my dad and ask him," she insisted.

I thought it was silly that I should have to call her father, but I could see that this was really important to her. So I knew that when the time came, I would have to make that call. And I was sure that time would come, because deep down I was certain I did want to marry her.

Anne I was really into this idea of courtship and "doing
it right." When I told John I wanted him to ask my
father's permission for us to marry, I knew my
dad would say "Fine, whatever." But I was determined that
everything between us be done appropriately.

Before going to visit my parents, John took me to meet his
family in Oregon. This was so energizing and exciting for me. I
met all his siblings—his dad and his second wife had had children—and I thought, *I could fit into this family.* They'd had so
many colorful experiences that one more colorful person in the
family was no big deal. In fact, I felt drab compared to them.
They were really, really fun. I just laughed at how well I fit in.

One day while we were there, we went to Multnomah Falls.
I didn't wear makeup because I figured I wouldn't see any of the
family members until later that night. In fact, I hadn't worn
much makeup on the trip anyway. So I did nothing more than
comb my hair.

For some reason, however, John seemed cold and distant.

"What's going on with you, John?" I asked after a while.
"Why are you so detached from me today?"

He said something about my makeup and some other
things I didn't understand. So I asked more questions.

His response led to a discussion about his own makeovers
during his drag stage and about his idea of "the ideal woman."
In short, he was comparing me to Candi and to his mom. I was
deeply hurt by his words.

As best I could, I tried to explain to him that his response
was very alienating. "John, I need you to love me just the way I
am," I insisted. "I need you to love *who* I am—with or without
my makeup."

We talked and argued and cried, but there wasn't much res-
olution. The incident grew into a huge conflict.

Once we arrived at my parents' house, the conflict escalated.
I was very tearful that first day. We went out to the car to talk
some more because I couldn't hold myself together in front of my

family. I couldn't pretend everything was fine when it wasn't.

"John," I said, "you know I really love you, but this whole thing could devastate me as a woman. You have to understand that I need to grow into myself, without the pressure of becoming this prototypical, perfect woman you've got in your mind. You're going to have to let me blossom into who I'm going to be. And I'm not promising you anything. I don't know how I'm going to end up, but I'm enjoying becoming a woman. I want the freedom to let God change me. But until He's finished, don't expect me to put on a performance for you!"

When John said something about wanting me to look my best for him, I realized he just wasn't hearing me.

"John, I really care about you," I reiterated. "But I can find a guy out there who'll love me as a tomboy. I can find somebody who won't care whether I wear makeup or not. And I love you enough to help you find a good woman. I'd be willing to do that."

John was shattered. He crumbled in front of me. He began to realize he loved me regardless and that he didn't want some little china doll anyway.

"Anne, it's not some 'image' I want—I want you," he affirmed. "I have this incredible love for you, and I didn't start loving you because you wore makeup."

We continued our trip, and we reconciled with each other. But I wasn't at all sure the problem was solved. This was a significant issue in John's life, spiritually and emotionally. Fortunately, we had a couple things working for us: John was willing to face the issue head-on, and I knew that, fundamentally, the issue wasn't about me—it was about him and his past. But it clearly had not been the right time for John to ask my dad for my hand in marriage.

John

Anne and I managed to get through the trip without utterly destroying our relationship. When we got back to San Rafael, I made an appointment for us to see Mike Riley. I was really heartsick, knowing that I could lose Anne over this.

As the three of us talked, I wept openly. I began to see that I was trying to put her into a role she was never intended to play. I had projected Candi on her and had tried to mold her into the "perfect" woman based on my glorified image of my mother. I was no longer dressing in drag, but I was still trying to create the ideal woman through makeup, hair, and clothing. Love wasn't about glamour, I realized, nor was it about being absorbed into someone else's identity. Real love was what I had with Anne, and I didn't want to lose it.

"Anne, will you forgive me for trying to make you into something you were never meant to be?" I asked.

"I forgive you, John," she assured me.

Then I prayed, "Lord, I cherish this woman and accept her for who she is. Please forgive me for trying to turn her into somebody else. Help me to always see her as the beautiful woman You made her to be, not as some other woman I might try to make her into."

After the meeting, we embraced in tears. Before long, Mike and I were talking about when, where, and how I should propose to Anne.

Anne John had his issues from the past to face, and I had mine. Before we could ever get engaged or married, I knew I had to deal with my fear that my father didn't really love me.

Every time my dad and I talked on the phone, our conversation was distant and unemotional, more like a father-son type of talk. My response had been to project the problem onto John—I had a tough time believing he truly loved me. John pointed this out to me and said that just as Candi had been a spiritual struggle for him, my doubt about my father was the same for me. And he was right.

During one conversation, I tried to talk to my father as a daughter, not a son. "Dad," I said, "I'm so excited! John and I are getting really serious. I even started looking at wedding dresses the other day. There was a beautiful one at a shop here that looked like it was made for a princess!"

There was a long pause. Then Dad said, "Well, how is your job going, Anne? I've purchased a new computer."

Then one night when John and I were visiting with my parents, I was all dressed up in makeup and a gorgeous, sophisticated, black-and-white dress. When I walked into the living room, my father hardly noticed me, and he never mentioned how beautiful I looked. He simply couldn't see me as a woman, and to me, it felt like rejection.

John and I came up with a plan of action in which I would directly ask my father about his feelings for me. One night I was on the phone with him and knew the time had come. I was afraid because he had never been vulnerable with me. But I managed to get the words out: "Dad, do you love me?"

Dad had always said *"We* love you," never "I love you." But now he was badly hurt that I'd asked the question, and his immediate response demonstrated his love for me. "I can't believe you're asking me this!" he exclaimed. "I sure do love you. Of course I do!"

"And do you *like* me, Dad?"

Again his response came without delay, "Of course I do. And I'm so proud of you." It was really a touching experience for me. I had rarely been able to face my deepest fears—I'd run away from them. But John's prodding helped me a great deal. He isn't afraid to face his fears, and he's taught me the same boldness.

John   One Saturday in December 1991, after a long talk with Mike Riley, I went home and nervously picked up the phone to call Anne's father in Spokane. After some opening small talk, I told him, "I guess you know that I really love Anne and want to marry her, Mr. Sutton.

I'm ready to propose to her. But before I do, I want to have your permission. Would it be all right with you and her mother if I ask for Anne's hand in marriage?"

He chuckled and replied, "It's a little old-fashioned for you to request our permission, John, but it's completely fine with us if you want to marry Anne."

"Thank you, Mr. Sutton!" I nearly shouted.

"And by the way," he added, "Anne's mother and I would be happy to pay for your wedding."

At the end of our conversation, satisfied that he was in agreement with what I was about to do, I hung up and went shopping for a ring.

A man named Dan who had gone through LIA many years before and was now married with three children owned a jewelry store in San Rafael. Someone had told me that he would help guys who were coming out of the gay lifestyle and getting married. So I went to him, told him about Anne and me, and explained that she likes diamonds. He seemed delighted by our story and said he had just gone to an estate sale and had something we might like. Then he pulled out a ring that had a center stone and 24 smaller diamonds around it. He offered it to me for a good price, and since I was sure Anne would love it, I bought it on the spot.

I took the ring home to Ohio with me at Christmas to show to my mom, grandmother, new stepdad, and everyone else who might share my joy. Before I left, I made plans to give it to Anne on New Year's Eve. I chose a wonderful restaurant, bought tickets to a big band concert where Rosemary Clooney would be singing, and found the perfect spot for the grand finale—my proposal. Everything was in place. All I had to do now was count the days until December 31.

Anne
_∞_
I spent Christmas with my parents, and a couple of days before New Year's, my father got a phone call from John in Ohio. This piqued my curiosity.

I wonder if he's going to ask me to marry him? I thought. *Why else would he have called Dad?*

Since John and I planned to celebrate New Year's Eve together, and since I suspected it might turn out to be a very special evening, I arranged for Mike Riley's wife to do my makeup and help me with my hair that day. More than anything else, I just wanted her to be there with me at such an important time.

I had a new, gorgeous, blue-silk dress, and by the time Mona was finished with me, I was ready for whatever might come to pass. John began our evening with dinner at a wonderful Italian restaurant, Il Fornaio in downtown San Francisco. It's in a beautiful location and the food was fabulous, but we were both nervous. We ate, but not much.

After dinner, John took me to a Rosemary Clooney concert. In her rich, vibrant voice, she sang one lovely romantic song after another. Somehow John had managed to get us front-row, center seats. As she performed "Our Love Is Here to Stay," Rosemary walked around the stage and noticed that John and I were holding hands. She recognized that we were young lovers and smiled at us with a sparkle in her eyes. My heart felt as big as the ocean, pounding like the surf. I couldn't turn my head to look at John's face.

Once the concert was over, John pretended not to know what he was going to do next. "Why don't we walk around Union Square?" he suggested, so we walked—for about an hour. My feet were starting to hurt, but we kept on walking, looking in every store window. I was beginning to think, *Maybe he's not going to ask me to marry him tonight! Why are we wasting all this time?*

Finally he said, "Well, I guess we should go." We walked to the van and started driving back to Marin County. As we approached the beautiful Palace of Fine Arts, which crowns a hill near the Golden Gate Bridge, I was wishing we could go back there now. We had been up there once before, and it had been so romantic.

Just then John said, "What should we do next?"

"I don't know," I answered. I was beginning to think I'd misread all the signals.

John
⌒◇⌒

Anne looked so radiant that I could hardly keep my eyes off her. After killing as much time as I possibly could in Union Square, we drove off toward the Golden Gate Bridge. And just before we got there, I acted as though I'd had an inspiration.

"Oh, Anne, there's the Palace of Fine Arts," I said. "Do you want to drive over there and just take a walk around?"

Her eyes shone with excitement. "Yes, let's!" she agreed.

We parked the car, and, as I walked over to open Anne's door, I checked my watch. We still had 45 minutes to go before midnight and the fireworks display that would be set off across the bay. I had hoped to wait until then to propose, but 45 minutes was a lot of time to kill, even in a spectacular setting like that. I tried to stall, but I knew the time had come.

I started to make my carefully planned speech, but to my chagrin, I found myself struggling with nervous laughter.

Anne looked troubled. "John, what's wrong?" she asked.

"Anne, there's something I need to tell you," I tried again. "I talked to your father on the phone a few days ago…" My voice was shaky, I was stammering, and for some absurd reason I was giggling like a 12-year-old.

"Oh? About what?"

"I asked him … how he would feel about you getting married. To me."

"You actually asked him? What did he say?"

I paused, trying to collect my thoughts and stop my absurd giggling.

"He said it was fine with him."

I was determined to do everything just the way Anne wanted, so I got down on one knee. Remembering the ring, I pulled out the velvet box from my pocket.

"Anne ..." I looked at her, suddenly afraid of what would come next. "Anne, will you marry me?"

Anne wrapped both arms around me. "Yes!" she cried. "Of course I'll marry you!"

In all the excitement, she had completely overlooked the small box I was clutching in my hand. "Anne," I said, "don't you want to see what's in the box?"

"Box? What box? Oh John, I'm so happy—I just want to hold you!"

Finally I couldn't stand it anymore. "Anne, for heaven's sake look in the box! Here!"

She slowly lifted the box's lid and peered inside. She gasped, momentarily speechless. "John, I can't believe this," she said. "It's so beautiful. Thank you so much. Wow! I don't know what to say."

"You did say yes, didn't you?"

"Of course I said yes, John. *Yes!* I'll marry you!"

Both of us had very shaky hands as I slipped the diamond on her finger. And just as we were about to admire it, the lights went out all around us. Then the fireworks began to go off across the bay, their brilliant colors mirrored in the dark waters. I took Anne in my arms, with the sounds of exploding pyrotechnics resounding in our ears. We held each other and kissed as the display lit up the night sky.

After walking back to the car hand in hand, I pulled a bouquet of roses out of the back and presented them to her. We looked at each other in near disbelief. We were engaged! We were going to get married! Unbelievable as it was, our new life together had just begun.

Anne
⌘

"I have a very special announcement to make," Pastor Mike Riley said the next Sunday. "Anne and John, would you please stand up?"

John and I glanced at each other and stood up, and Mike

told everybody, "I am delighted to announce that John and Anne are engaged to be married!"

Instantly, the entire congregation began to cheer and shout and applaud. John and I were hugged, kissed, and congratulated by nearly every person there, and the celebration went on long after the service ended. Finally we walked outside and caught our breath. It was now official. We were engaged, and everyone knew it.

Before long, though, we came down off the high. The closer we got to the wedding, the more we argued about everything imaginable—from dishes to decorating, from the kind of picture frames we liked (I liked wood and he liked gold) to whether we should go into Victoria's Secret together to buy items for my trousseau.

"Oh, my gosh, this is really intimate wear," I remarked, embarrassed by the risqué bras and panties displayed so boldly in the window. "You know I can't walk through there with you right now."

John was patient with me all along the way. He knew I needed time to feel comfortable in our relationship. I felt so honored by the way he respected and valued me. His consideration greatly strengthened my security as a woman.

As we progressed through our engagement period, we became increasingly excited about the wedding. We made all the plans ourselves because we wanted it to be the most wonderful wedding any of our friends and acquaintances had ever attended. More importantly, we wanted it to be a visible testimony to God's amazing work in our lives. How better could we announce to the world that He is still in the business of doing miracles?

John

Our engagement was a time of great joys and great challenges. Anne and I both took our approaching marriage seriously. We wanted the most beautiful wedding ceremony ever planned. We also wanted a happily-ever-after fairytale wedding, but we knew that wouldn't happen without a huge amount of prayer and preparation. Needless to say, our feelings ran high, and those months were not without their emotional bruises. Anne and I are both very sensitive, and it wasn't difficult for us to hurt each other, especially during such a stressful time.

In my quiet moments, I hoped and prayed that I had grown enough spiritually to be a good husband. Now and then I wrestled with the thought that I might not be successful in a heterosexual relationship. Anne, too, had doubts and fears, so we entered into some serious premarital counseling with Mike Riley. We focused on communication skills and continued to reaffirm our commitment to each other.

Although the preparations for the wedding were stressful, they were also exciting and creatively satisfying. We had so many choices to make about the bridal party, the vows, the invitations, and all sorts of other details. We brought different tastes to the table, and sometimes the negotiations over "how it should be done" were more than a little heated. Fortunately, with Mike's wit and wisdom easing the tension, we made it through without serious incidents.

I was greatly encouraged by the advice and assurance of some friends who were former homosexuals. Each of them had married and had remained happily so, and they provided me with both practical suggestions and a good measure of optimism that everything would work out fine.

It was amazing to me that I was having "father-son" talks with ex-gay men about the female anatomy, the sexual response of women, and the romance and intimacy a man and a woman share on their honeymoon. Frank Worthen reminded me, "Your marriage to Anne is a wonderful thing. God has ordained it. And you don't need to worry: He's not going to abandon you in the moment when you need Him the most."

The months flew by in a blur of activity, and at last our wedding day dawned bright and beautiful. As I thought about the events that were about to unfold, I was suddenly aware of God's presence. His love seemed to fill my room, and a warm sense of anticipation overwhelmed me with joy and hope. God had seen us through so much for so long. And now here we were, ready to embark on a new life together with Him. His grace and goodness would be with us for the rest of our lives. I knew it, and I already felt it in my heart.

I dressed for the day—formal tie and tails—and made my way to the place we had chosen for the ceremony, the San Francisco Theological Seminary. Last-minute details rushed through my mind, but when I caught sight of Stewart Chapel's steeple, the reality of what was about to happen struck me. I started to feel nervous, wondering how the ceremony would go and what the honeymoon would be like.

One after another, the various participants and members of the bridal party began to arrive. Mike Riley, who would be performing the ceremony, greeted me joyfully. I was glad to see his friendly face, but I felt even more anxious as he began to banter with me about the occasion. Sensing my apprehension, he said, "Come with me. I'm going to pray for you."

Mike took me aside, put his arm around me, and started to pray for God's peace and blessing to surround me. I'll never forget his prayer:

"Bless this day, Lord, and make it a testimony to Your love and grace. Prepare every person who will attend this wedding, that their hearts would be changed by what they see and moved by what they experience. Most of all, Lord, I pray for Anne and John, that the love You have placed in their hearts for each other would grow and flourish and bear much fruit for Your kingdom."

Love Won Out

Anne

Our wedding day morning, my bridesmaids and I all went out to get manicures and pedicures. "We'll do it together," I told them, "and we'll all have a great time."

I'd asked Beverly, the good-hearted woman who had done my makeup at the Emporium, to come and help us all get ready for the ceremony. Three out of five members of my bridal party had come out of the gay lifestyle, and never before had they been professionally made up. We had our hair done by some beauticians in our church, and they made a point of telling me that they felt honored to be involved.

Before long, we were all combed, sprayed, powdered, and glossed to perfection, and it was time for me to put on my wedding dress. The gown was breathtaking—pure white, with softly puffed sleeves and a wide, graceful skirt. The top was embroidered with pearls and beads, and a six-foot train streamed out behind me. My veil flowed from a band of pearls and beads that perfectly matched the dress's bodice.

We had arranged to have our pictures taken before the wedding. When I arrived at the hotel lobby to pick up my family, my father was nowhere to be found. I called his room, but he wasn't there. My mother didn't even know where he was, though she was sure he didn't have his tux on—it was still hanging in their closet. I struggled with my disappointment as she tracked him down, eventually finding him in my brother's hotel room, watching a ball game on TV.

Fortunately, Dad rose to the occasion. He seemed to feel genuinely sorry about his poor sense of timing, and he hurried to get ready. He finally showed up in the lobby just a half hour late. The limousine had been waiting outside as long as I'd been waiting in the lobby, and the thought had crossed my mind more than once that I should leave for the chapel without him. Fortunately, I didn't. But I felt dishonored by his action. It seemed to me that he didn't care enough to be on time for my wedding, and I couldn't understand why.

All the time we were taking pictures, waiting for first one group and then another to show up, Beverly was there beside me, freshening my makeup and ensuring that every aspect of my appearance was perfect, right to the last minute. She was so sweet, and I suddenly realized that she had almost adopted me as her daughter. Her entire focus was on making me beautiful. I was awed by her acceptance of me. My past didn't matter to her. She wasn't offended by anything except the possibility that I would look less than my best for the biggest day of my life.

John The organist began to play "His Sheep May Safely Graze." By then, both my mother and Anne's were in their seats. Soon it would be time for the groomsmen to enter the sanctuary. My best man was John Smid, who had been my house leader when I'd first arrived at Love in Action. He had seen me through every aspect of my process of change. Now he would stand beside me as I took this new step.

"My legs are about to collapse, John," I whispered as we headed for the door. "You'll have to catch me if I fall."

He turned and smiled. "I'm right behind you, John," he assured me, "and you're going to be just fine."

I glanced around the chapel and realized that hundreds of people were there—every seat was taken. The scent of fresh flowers, the radiance of softly glowing candles, and the sight of so many friendly faces lifted my heart. I was suddenly gripped with joy—God had done the impossible, and Anne and I were there to prove it to each other and to the world.

Everyone was smiling with delight, and in gratitude I

breathed a prayer: *Lord, I never want to forget this moment. Help me to remember each sight and sound, every face—even the fragrance of the flowers.*

The LIA men were seated at my right—I had noticed them sitting together as I walked in. To my shock—and amusement—with a perfect sense of choreography they all donned hot-pink, triangle-shaped sunglasses at the same time. The audience broke into laughter, and in spite of the sacredness of the wedding, so did I.

As Purcell's "Trumpet Voluntary" began, a white runner was rolled down the center aisle. In the back of the sanctuary, French doors swung open, and Anne's bridesmaids began to move slowly down the aisle, dressed in flowing, blue-satin gowns.

Anne's sister—also her matron of honor—came in last, deeply moved by the occasion and the beauty of the church. She wept as she walked in, and I reached out and touched her arm as she went by me. She smiled at me, then took her place and stood facing the audience, her face gleaming with tears.

The music stopped. The French doors closed. The room fell silent. Outside, I heard the chapel bells strike five times. The moment had finally arrived.

Anne Without John's knowledge, I had arranged to have the French doors closed after the bridesmaids entered and took their places. A hush fell across the sanctuary. When the doors opened again, it was as if a beautiful princess were walking down the aisle. The moment was incredible. I could hardly believe it was me.

As my father and I entered, John caught his breath and began to cry. He looked over at my sister, who was already in tears. I swept down the aisle, my cathedral train flowing dramatically behind me. It was an unforgettable experience for us all.

Our friend Mark sang the song "My Redeemer," which had

won my heart to John when I first heard him sing it. John and I were facing the singer, and I couldn't help but mouth the words. It was such an appropriate song because God had done just what the lyric said He would do—He had made promises, and He had fulfilled them. He had made commitments to me, and He had brought them to completion. Everything that had happened was beyond my understanding, beyond my capability, and had been accomplished in spite of myself.

I was crying, John was crying, and the whole audience was in tears. Some of them weren't even Christian believers. Others were men and women who had decided to leave the gay lifestyle to follow Jesus. Still others were family members who knew where we had been. But all of us had at least one thing in common—we were moved to tears by the beauty and wonder of the occasion.

John   "Dearly beloved," Mike began, "we are gathered today in the sight of God and this company to join together these two people in holy matrimony...."

I led Anne up the steps to the main altar, her arm through mine. We turned to face each other, and we held hands as we repeated our vows to each other.

"John, repeat after me," Mike said. "I, John, take you, Anne ..."

Anne and I looked into each other's eyes as we spoke the words that would bind us together for the rest of our lives.

Mike struggled to hold back tears as he spoke to each of us with love in his heart. At the end of his sermon, he encouraged us to stay committed to the Lord: "Anne and John, your marriage will only be as strong as your personal relationship with Jesus Christ. As long as each of you keeps Him as the center of your life, you will be able to weather any storm."

Finally he said the words we had been waiting all day to hear: "And now, by the power vested in me, I pronounce you husband and wife. And what God has joined together, let no man put asunder."

Mike smiled at me and nodded. "John, you may kiss your bride!"

I lifted Anne's veil, and everyone laughed as I tossed it back, took her in my arms, and kissed her wholeheartedly. The audience burst into applause as we turned and faced them, and just then Mike's voice filled our ears with the wonderful announcement, "Ladies and gentlemen, I now have the extreme pleasure of introducing to you ... *Mr. and Mrs. John Paulk!*"

The applause nearly drowned out the recessional. I felt such a sense of relief and triumph as we started down the aisle that I raised my fist and shouted, "We did it! We did it!"

I can't imagine a more exuberant scene than the outpouring of love and good wishes we received after the ceremony. Our first embraces were for our mothers and the rest of our family members. My mom held me close and said, "John, I love you so much. And I can't tell you how proud I am of you." Then others showered us with blessings and congratulations. Eventually, we settled into a stretch limousine for the drive to the San Rafael Embassy Suites Hotel, where we continued our celebration at the reception.

Anne My friend Renee, one of my bridesmaids, had a vision during our wedding ceremony. As a picture formed in her mind, she saw angels hovering above us in the chapel while we said our vows. And when Mike Riley—who had loved us like a father through this whole process—introduced us as man and wife, the angels, luminous with joy, held their swords high above their heads and shouted, "Victory! Victory!"

In this spirit of triumph and joy, we greeted our guests at the reception. We had dinner for 300 people, and afterward John and I stepped onto the dance floor. We had chosen a song by

Rosemary Clooney, "Our Love Is Here to Stay"—one of the songs we had heard her perform on New Year's Eve. John and I danced together during that special song, and then we danced with our family members. The other guests then joined us for the rest of the evening.

Our church had never seen anything quite like this event, and that's exactly what we wanted. We had dreamed that all our family and friends from church and Love in Action could come, enjoy themselves, and not have to settle for punch and cookies or a potluck dinner. We wanted to treat them like royalty, and that's what we did.

It was a such a magnificent celebration! And that's just the way John and I wanted it to be, because we had plenty of reason to celebrate.

John   When the party began to wind down and the time came for us to leave for our honeymoon, I started to feel nervous again. For months, Anne and I had enjoyed emotional and spiritual closeness in our relationship, but now we would be entering a new level of intimacy. For me, fear of failure was almost as strong as my sense of excitement and anticipation.

But by now we had said good-bye to everybody. And just as I glanced around the room to make sure I hadn't missed thanking anyone, Anne looked at me a little shyly and said, "Don't you think it's time we should be leaving?"

My dad had booked us into the bridal suite at the Sheraton Palace, a newly restored, turn-of-the-century hotel in San Francisco. It was elegant and well prepared for nervous honeymooners.

After check-in, I carried Anne across the threshold and into our room. Fine woods and lavish furnishings greeted us. The centerpiece of the suite was an enormous four-poster bed. As Anne put on her delicate, white-silk peignoir, I turned on some music and lit a couple of candles. Once she emerged, I took her in my arms and held her close to my heart.

We weren't in any hurry, and in the hours and days that followed, my anxieties about our physical relationship were replaced by my growing love for Anne.

Anne   I was as nervous as John. I was anxious about leaving the party, about going to the hotel, and about being sexually intimate. We had already decided we weren't going to pressure each other to perform that night. We knew we would be on such a high and yet so exhausted that we wouldn't be at our best, no matter how much we wanted to be together. It would be foolish for us to expect our wedding night to be the ultimate experience.

When we arrived at the hotel, the staff delivered sparkling cider and raspberries—simply elegant and delectable. The staff treated us like a king and queen. And once we were alone together, we spent hours and hours holding each other and kissing each other so tenderly, so lovingly. That night was so wonderfully intimate that it was hard to imagine that consummating our love would be even better. But we would soon find out that it was much better indeed.

John   The next morning, we got up late and were served breakfast in our room. After a late check-out, we went to the apartment we had rented. All our presents had been taken there, including one gift Anne hadn't yet seen—a Queen Anne-style jewelry box. Inside it was a brass plate bearing this engraved message: "To my beautiful bride on our wedding day, July 19, 1992."

Anne had just opened my wedding present when the phone rang. It was Vicky's husband, Bruce, my brother-in-law.

"Are you sitting down?" he began. "I'm about to give you the best wedding present of all."

"What are you talking about?" I asked. "What is it?"

"After the wedding reception was over, your mom and Tom [her husband] joined Vicky and me in our hotel room. They were just amazed by everything that had happened and couldn't quite understand it all. I told them that the source of all the wonderful things that had happened to you and Anne was Jesus Christ. I explained His plan of salvation to them and asked if they wanted to accept Jesus into their hearts. And John, they did! Both of them prayed with us to receive the Lord!"

He was right. The wedding had been blessed with joy, vision, and wonder. But nothing could touch this. God had used the transformation of our lives to bring my mother and her husband into His kingdom. We couldn't have asked for a better gift.

Anne
◌⟡◌
We had the most romantic honeymoon in Hawaii. That whole week, we didn't argue one time. Our experiences together were fun, sensuous, and tender. I enjoyed the fact that when I woke up in the morning after making love, I didn't feel any separation from God. I didn't feel any regret. I didn't feel as if I needed to repent.

Our lovemaking felt so right and good, as if He were putting His stamp of approval on us. I could sense God saying, "Delight in each other. I made all this for you to enjoy."

I wrote in my journal, "John and I were sitting in lawn chairs, watching the sunset, and he fell asleep on my lap. My heart was so full of thankfulness. And I asked God to strengthen me in my weak areas: believing that God and John love me. When John woke up, he was so happy that he had married me and God had finally given him his other half. Wow, what a wonderful and fast answer to prayer! I love being married to John!"

John

Our honeymoon was one of the happiest, most fulfilling times of our lives. So many fears and doubts were swept away in a tide of passion and pleasure. It was God's gift to both of us, and we received it with sheer gratitude. We exchanged no cross words. Instead, we took long walks on the beach and long naps, just enjoying being together 24 hours a day and bonding like never before. But all too quickly it was time to leave, so after seven blissful days, we returned to the "real" world.

When we got back home, it started to become known publicly that we had married after coming out of homosexual backgrounds. An opportunity soon came to appear on ABC's *Good Morning America*. After that, invitations to be interviewed by national media arrived almost every week. *The 700 Club* and various other Christian programs called, as did *The Oprah Winfrey Show*, along with people making documentaries.

As a result of all this sudden media exposure, we became a celebrity couple of sorts, and our relationship was "on stage." At the same time, like all newly married couples, we were trying to merge two lives, two ways of doing things. At age 29, we were both pretty set in our ways. We soon found ourselves bickering about little things like which pictures to hang and where.

This "fighting" led us to start worrying that our gay backgrounds were the root cause of the problem. So we decided to get counseling.

As we sat in the counselor's office that day and explained the disputes we were having and the nature of our histories, he laughed. Then he said, "Oh, if you two only knew how normal you are! Your problems aren't really problems at all." He went on to explain that our spats weren't about being gay but simply about a man and woman getting to know each other. Because we knew ourselves so well after all the therapy we'd been through, he added, we actually had a stronger foundation to our marriage than most couples.

What we *did* need to learn, he went on, was how to communicate better. Each of us had to understand how to translate what the other was saying, especially when we had disagreements. Again, this was all part of the normal process for newlyweds.

We took delight in hearing that and having our fears removed. We had been bothered by how different we were and how we seemingly couldn't agree on anything. But the counselor convinced us that we needed to stop trying to make the other person just like us and instead let our strengths and weaknesses complement each other. We had thought that to get along we had to be the same; he explained, "Let your differences be your strength. Let the other enhance what's lacking in you. That's how you'll build a strong marriage."

As time went by and Anne felt more secure in my love and in her understanding that even when I got mad I still loved her, her femininity blossomed. She developed an inner strength and beauty that showed on the outside. The feminine became familiar to her and not foreign, just as the masculine became familiar to me.

We learned to talk through everything no matter how insignificant or how enormous it seemed. We learned to listen, to discuss, and to forgive. We learned to understand the old, tangled motives that sometimes put up new, unpleasant shoots of growth. Most of all, we learned to say, "I'm sorry, I love you, and I want to try again." With God's help, nothing was impossible for us to work through.

Anne   Within the first three months after the wedding, Mona Riley asked me to lead worship at a women's retreat. I had always dreamed of using my musical talents. But although I loved singing and playing my guitar, performing solo in public scared me to death.

Among the ex-gay women in our church was a young woman whom several of us were mentoring. She was a drummer—a good one—but she was also very feminine. During one of our rehearsals, she approached me and began to flatter me about my singing. Unexpectedly, I found myself having a sexual response to her and, of course, feeling tremendously ashamed of it. There I was, newly married, with most things going well, and suddenly this attraction arose, seemingly out of nowhere.

My reaction, after the initial flattery wore off, was *I don't want this*. So I talked it over with John. "You can share a little bit with me, but I also want you to talk with your friend Sheila," he said. "You can really pour it all out to her." So that's what I did— I told John some of what happened, and he pinpointed a couple things he saw. Then I talked to Sheila, and the three of us together discussed it in detail.

I came to understand that my physical response to this young woman was a crutch. Because music was a new area I had moved into and I was feeling so insecure about leading the worship at the retreat, I had subconsciously reached back for an old, familiar form of security. I had responded to her flattery on an emotional and sexual level, as if that would solve my problem.

The logic—or lack of it—was stunning. I was behaving as if her flattery would solve all my problems. I was functioning as if, were I to have sex with her, I would feel much better about getting up and leading worship in front of a bunch of women! It was utterly absurd, but that's the way my emotional habits had been formed. They clearly needed further reforming.

As I faced up to my insecurity and examined what was really going on in my mind, that attraction faded completely away. And the three of us—John, Sheila, and I—had a good laugh about it. It was out in the open, it was not secretive, and— best of all—it was over.

John also helped me learn another important lesson during the first year of our marriage. We were often on the phone with our families. I talked to my dad frequently about my achievements at work and my various activities. One day when I had just hung up after talking to Dad, John observed, "Anne, you're talking to your dad like you're his son. You're not talking to him about your sensitivities, the female things in your life, or how you're blossoming as a woman. That's what you're really excited about, Anne. You're not excited about your job. But you're talking to your dad about it as if it were all that mattered to you."

"Yeah, you're right," I told him. "It's funny, but I've never noticed that before. I'm always coming into my dad's world to try to relate to him. And he has never once come into mine."

The next time I talked to Dad on the phone, I began to tell him about what John and I dreamed of doing someday, how I had responded emotionally to something, and how much I'd love to have a baby. I chattered on and on about the feminine things I was really interested in, and Dad was stone silent on the other end. He didn't even know how to say, "Oh, that's interesting." He was speechless until I switched the talk to work issues.

From that time on, I started to be myself with Dad. I was a woman, and he would just have to deal with it. That was a good process for me. And ultimately, it was good for both of us.

John   During the latter part of 1993, Anne and I realized
ᥫᨆ   that it was time we moved away from San Rafael in general and LIA in particular. We had many wonderful friends there, and we'd learned a new way of life, especially under the kind hand of Pastor Mike Riley. But we were still absorbed with ex-gay ministry, and our identities as ex-gays were too narrow and confining.

Our exposure to national media was ongoing—by now we had appeared on dozens of programs, as well as on local news and talk shows. All this had brought us to a point where we were too easily recognized on the street and too well known in our circle of friends and acquaintances. We thought it would be good to start over in a new place with more anonymity.

Both our families lived in the Northwest, and my dad was more than willing to help us get resettled in Portland, Oregon, near him and my siblings. He and his wife, Sue, invited us to come live with them while we looked for a place of our own. Since he hadn't been able to have me live with him when I was a boy, this was a way he could do something for me now. It was a loving gesture, one that moved me deeply, and we agreed to settle there for a while.

We left San Rafael just before Christmas, and it was a tearful good-bye. Our friends came to see us off, and they wept as we pulled away in our U-Haul truck. LIA had been our family for five years, but now we had a family of our own—each other—and we needed to grow together as one in Christ.

Anne In Portland, we were determined to be just John
⟨∞⟩ and Anne. We wanted to work on our relationship without the world watching. This was a profoundly healing time for John—his father provided us a place to stay, food, and anything else we needed. With every gesture, he seemed to be saying, "Son, I love you and want to give you what I never could before."

Those were special times for me, too. John's dad treated me like a daughter. In some ways, it was easier for him to demonstrate his affection for me than for his own daughters, because he had no history with me. He really extended himself to show he loved me.

Within a couple of months of moving, I found a job training people how to use various computer software programs. I'd been introduced to this line of work toward the end of our time in California, and I stayed with the company for the next several years.

Early in 1994, a friend came up to visit us. She kept talking about her pregnancy and all the symptoms she was feeling. I told her, "Well, I'm pretty sure we're not pregnant." Then, after she left, I realized that I had some of the same symptoms she'd mentioned. More importantly, I suddenly realized my period was late.

It was February 14—Valentine's Day—when I said, "John, I have a feeling we should get a pregnancy test kit."

We bought the test, I took it, and it came out positive. At first our hearts soared, but within minutes we were terrified that it wasn't true. So we went and got another test. John went back every two seconds to make sure the blue line was still there. It was true—both tests said the same thing.

We told John's dad and his wife. I had this little doll stuffed under my shirt and walked around proud of myself. For us, the news was a Valentine's present from God, a very special gift. We could hardly believe it was true. John checked the test sticks all night long and even the next day to make sure they hadn't changed!

We were so elated that we ran around telling everyone. I called my family; John called his. "Mom," he said, "I'm going to be a father!"

"And I'm going to be a mother!" I added, trying to make my voice heard through the receiver.

The next night when John came home, I said, "You know, it's a miracle I made it home in one piece. I drove to and from work in a daze."

"I know," John responded with a laugh. "I can hardly believe it's really happening. Me—a father! When I think about it, I feel a whole new rush of masculinity and healing."

The next five days were filled with looking up baby stores in the Yellow Pages and traveling throughout the Portland area, picking out a theme for the baby's room and finding matching sheets, curtains, and wallpaper. We wanted to get a head start in choosing what we would purchase for our new little one. We were radiant with expectation, and it showed.

John's stepmother took one look at us and said, "You two are just glowing with happiness. I've never seen anybody so happy about a baby."

"Nobody could be any happier than we are," John agreed, giving me a hug.

Then, five days later, I started to bleed. A couple of days after that, I began to cramp. That night, the pain woke me up three times out of a sound sleep. Scared and helpless, John called the doctor, and he told us to go to the emergency room.

After we were admitted, a technician did an ultrasound. Afterward, he wouldn't tell us a thing. "Just wait in the emergency room," he said, avoiding our eyes, "and I'll have someone interpret it for you there."

So we sat, hoping with all our hearts that our baby was all right. By then I was about eight weeks pregnant. Finally the E.R. doctor called us and walked alongside us to one of the little rooms.

"Were you guys trying to get pregnant?" she asked matter-of-factly.

"No, we weren't," I answered.

"Well then, I guess you were going to have an abortion anyway," she said bluntly, writing something on a chart.

And that's how we found out the baby was dead.

We were stunned. We felt as if someone had knocked the emotional wind out of us.

As we followed the doctor to the room, my heart lagged behind. I was having a hard time comprehending what she had just told us. I felt I was in a time warp, moving in slow motion. As she continued to give us information, I couldn't even listen. She rambled on, but one phrase echoed again and again in my head:

"The baby is dead. The baby is dead. *The baby is dead.*"

I was trembling with shock and disbelief.

"Oh, God! It just can't be!"

John and I looked at each other. We couldn't process that thought. "So exactly what are you saying?" John asked the doctor.

"Oh, they hadn't told you yet?" she replied, still as disinterested as ever. She took my blood pressure and asked me if I wanted a D & C right then. John and I looked at each other again, and by now tears were welling up in our eyes. We began to sob in each other's arms.

The woman had no compassion for us. She finally said, "Well, I guess you two would like to be alone."

After she disappeared, John held me close. "Anne, I'm so sorry this has happened," he consoled.

"I'm sorry, too," I managed.

Our grief was unfathomable. In our excitement, we'd looked at all kinds of stuffed animals, baby clothes, and nursery decorations—even diapers—that we wanted to buy. Now we learned that the baby had been dead for several weeks. The process of miscarriage had simply been delayed. At the time, it felt like a cruel cosmic joke.

Still, I wasn't ready to do anything about it. I couldn't bear to have a D & C because somehow I still cherished a thread of hope that maybe the baby wasn't dead after all. We believed in miracles, didn't we? Since neither of us knew anything about this experience, we desperately wanted to get out of that horrible place and away from the ice-cold presence of the doctor. Once she was finished taking my blood pressure, I told her, "No, I'm not interested in a D & C. We're going home."

"Well," she said in her frosty, detached way, "when you start bleeding, come back to the E.R. and check in. And if you see any parts of the fetus when you go to the bathroom, please bring them in."

Shocked and devastated, we went home. As I began bleeding more severely, I grew fearful that I would see something. I couldn't face the prospect of seeing bits and pieces of this baby that we had treasured. A day and a half later, the bleeding was more severe. I told John, "This is serious. The cramping has intensified. Let's go. I'm ready."

The D & C was terribly painful. I remember grabbing hold of the table with both hands and trying to stifle my cries. John was outside the room; they wouldn't let him in. He heard me, though, because I couldn't help but cry out from the pain. Afterward, we went home and collapsed. The ordeal was over, but we had lost a part of ourselves in the process.

John   I really struggled with blaming God for the miscarriage. My emotions were so battered that part of me almost wanted to renounce my faith. Anne's faith didn't waver as much as mine, at least not at that point.

We grieved for months and months. We had lost someone dear to us, and our hopes seemed to have died with him. To make matters worse, we tried and tried, but Anne couldn't get pregnant again. We started going to a fertility doctor, trying to figure out Anne's ovulation cycle. We followed the doctor's instructions to the letter, but still no baby.

Gradually, time did its healing work, our spirits lifted, and we got distracted by a new project—finding and moving into a home of our own. Phil, who directed an Exodus-affiliated ministry, mentioned to us that he was remodeling an 80-year-old farmhouse, and he thought we might be interested in it.

When we walked into the house, we immediately knew we wanted to buy it. It exuded all the charm and character of a large country home, with plenty of room for the many guests we hoped to entertain. We were able to work out the financial details with Phil, and in October 1994, Anne and I moved into our dream house. We had plenty to do, and the process of decorating went on for months. But it kept us occupied, and before long we were able to settle in, delighted with the outcome of our hard work and feeling very much at home.

I was working for a Christian medical ministry by this time and had taken a much-needed two-and-a-half year break from ex-gay ministry. But in May 1995, John Smid called to ask if I would be willing to run for election to the Exodus board of directors. Anne and I talked it over, and I decided to attend the

Exodus conference in San Diego. While there, I was honored to be elected to an Exodus board position for the next three years.

A few months later, Anne and I were contacted by two businessmen who had been supporting the Portland Fellowship, the local Exodus outreach, for many years. They had followed us since our days in San Rafael, watching our interviews on TV and reading those in print, and had been impressed with how we expressed ourselves and articulated the message of coming out of homosexuality. Now they wanted to fund a position for me with the Portland Fellowship so I could spread the message full-time to the media and the community at large.

The timing was awesome, as I had been sensing the Lord's leading to get back into active ex-gay ministry. So with their backing, I set up my new job as public relations director with the Portland Fellowship. More media opportunities came, including one to be interviewed by Leslie Stahl for CBS's highly rated *60 Minutes.*

All this was confirmation that God was, indeed, calling us back to ex-gay ministry. He still had a purpose for us on a national scale in spite of the recent death of our child.

Anne In August 1995, I was driving across the country,
ᔕᕼ   helping one of my friends move her belongings.
       As we stopped beside the road one day, I looked
up into the sky and saw an unusual cloud formation. It looked like a baby. *How strange,* I thought, *I've never seen a cloud like that before. I wonder…*

Meanwhile, John was in prayer at home, pleading with God. He was in tears, crying out, *God, please give us a baby! Why won't You give us a baby?*

We wanted to be parents so badly, it hurt. We were almost desperate because we felt wonderfully connected to each other as husband and wife, and we wanted everything God could provide us as a married couple. Becoming parents seemed to us like the next step in our complete healing from our pasts.

We had experienced incredible and unexpected joy during our first pregnancy. Now that the disappointment had diminished a little, we longed for fulfillment of our deep, God-ordained desire to enlarge our family. We knew it was a good thing to want to share our lives with children, to nurture them and help them grow. But instead of seeing our dream come true, all we had experienced was frustration, disappointment, and a heartbreaking loss like nothing we'd ever known.

Not long thereafter, I learned that I was pregnant again. Our hopes soared, especially after we passed the ninth week of pregnancy. But then, like a terrible flashback, I started to bleed again. And even though we now had a wonderful Christian doctor and a supportive, prayerful medical team on our side, we had another miscarriage in September 1995.

Neither John nor I handled this tragedy especially well. John really struggled, possibly even more than I did. I remember praying, *God, John feels as if You've put a carrot in front of us and then yanked it away. It's so cruel. Lord, I know that's not really the way You are, but that's how it feels. I need You to comfort John and give him some kind of vision of Your love.*

Not long thereafter, still struggling, I attended a women's retreat. We were going through Kay Arthur's material about the names of God. One of the names was *El-Elyon*—the God who sees. Something about that name moved me to tears, and I left the meeting.

I was really hurting, and I needed to unburden my heart to God. So I walked around outside, crying and praying, *Lord, I really wish I was a mother. I don't have any promises from You that I'm ever going to have a child. John and I just long to be parents. We want to really love a child together and have our own family.*

I wouldn't say I was resentful, but I had been deeply hurt and still felt tremendous grief. I kept bringing back to God my unfulfilled longing to be a mother.

God doesn't owe me anything, I told myself again and again.

I'm His child, gladly His servant, and He's sovereign. I kept trying to surrender my longings, but I couldn't bring myself to stop asking for this good gift.

Once I'd walked around outside for a while, I found a quiet place where I could talk with God alone. The emotional longing brought up tears before I could even begin.

"Lord," I prayed aloud, "You are God. You've blessed John and me with so much and in so many ways. We've learned to trust You in difficult areas in the past—in jobs, moving, sexuality, friendships, and finances. And You have proved Yourself trustworthy. I know having children is in Your hands. Your Word says, 'Delight yourself in the LORD and he will give you the desires of your heart. Commit your way to the LORD; trust in him' (Psalm 37:4-5). I can't seem to surrender my desire to be a mother, even though I'm trying. Help me, Lord, to make my desires an offering, not a demand."

And with that, I stopped praying and waited to hear from the only One who could touch the deepest part of my heart and longings.

In those quiet moments, God never said, *I'm going to make you a mother.* But He did say, *I am the God who sees.* At that very moment, I knew that He saw my pain, that He hadn't turned His eyes away from me. He was experiencing the loss with me. It was a life-changing insight, and I left from that conference feeling whole. He had helped me understand that no matter what was lacking, He was in it with me. And with Him beside me, I knew I could go on.

John   As 1996 began, I realized I was having a hard time praying and reading my Bible. I was mad at God over the death of our babies. I felt rejected. I felt, actually, like a dangling marionette that God was just playing some cruel game with. I had an overwhelming, almost physical desire to be a parent, and the hurt because of the loss of our two children was excruciating. Sitting through the dedication of other people's babies in church was agony; Anne usually had to get up and walk out. So I often found myself wrestling with God, crying in despair, *Won't You ever let us be parents?*

After months of struggle and despair, after more tears than I could number and more prayers than I could remember, it was as if the heavy, dense mist that had separated me from God was removed. In an instant, God gave me an awareness of something I'd never even thought about before. He showed me, in my spirit, a time when I would be reunited with our two little babies.

God said to my heart, *I know you're hurting, John. But please remember that the first ones you're going to see when you come to heaven are your two babies. They're with Me right now, and they're never going to experience sin or death. I'm raising them, and I'm a perfect parent. So don't worry, you still have the family members you thought you had lost.*

It was a tremendous comfort to know I would see our unborn children again. At last I was able to release our unborn children into His care, and for the first time in months, I felt peace. Finally I could go on, no longer estranged from God.

The Lord had some important things for us to do. Media interest in our love story had intensified. After I wrote a letter about our marriage to *The Wall Street Journal*, Anne and I appeared on *ABC Evening News* with Peter Jennings, we were on *60 Minutes*, and we were interviewed for several national publications.

Now and then someone would ask about our efforts to have a baby, and we just tried to smile and let the person know we were doing just fine, thank you very much, baby or no baby. We had stopped taking Anne's temperature, deciding that we wouldn't concern ourselves with conception, and we set aside our dreams about having our first child. By then that wasn't such a difficult change of mind. For us, pregnancy meant heartbreak, and we'd had enough of that for a while.

Anne John and I gave up the idea of being parents. We
     got rid of the temperature charts and stopped
     thinking about my ovulation cycle. I'd had a dye
test, John had taken a sperm count, and, as far as that was concerned, everything was working right. But we just had to let go.
We prayed, *Lord, it's in Your hands, and we're not going to try to
control it anymore.* We were content with our walk with God,
with being hospitable to people, and with doing whatever work
God put in front of us.

Then, in March 1996, I realized I was pregnant again.

Every time I went to the bathroom after that, I was afraid I
would see bleeding again. And day after day I prayed, *Lord, I'm
really scared. But I just want to thank You for each and every day You
let me hold this baby in my womb.*

We passed the 12-week mark. Everybody at the doctor's
office seemed to know about our past miscarriages, and they
did all they could to encourage us, such as winking at us when
we walked in. Meanwhile, I was getting bigger and bigger as
our fears grew smaller and smaller. Dr. Timothy Stewart, my
OB-GYN, was a gift from God. If I felt insecure, he'd have me in
the office that very day to do another ultrasound. He did it simply to encourage me, and he didn't even charge us for it. It was
a time of high hopes and spiritual growth. John and I were
beginning to be really excited.

John At 22 weeks, during one of the ultrasound tests, I
     looked at the screen and observed with a laugh,
     "The baby's so big!"

"Yes, and everything looks just the way it's supposed to,"
Dr. Stewart assured us. "All the fingers and toes are there. You
can even see the mouth moving."

As we watched in wonder, the baby squirmed. Now there
was no denying it—I could see for myself that our baby was
alive and well.

"Can you tell if it's a boy or a girl?" I asked, suddenly curious.

When Dr. Stewart quietly said, "You have a little boy," I was stunned. For the first time, my role as a father to a son became real to me. "I have a son," I told myself again and again in the days that followed.

I reflected back on the problems I had faced as a small boy: the taunts and jeers on the playground; the inappropriate behavior of teenage baby-sitters; the exposure to pornography. Could I protect my son from all that? Most of all, could I help him embrace his maleness from day one so that he would never face the gender confusion I had been through for so much of my life? The responsibilities that lay ahead seemed enormous. But my joy was greater yet, and my confidence was that God, who had begun a good work in me, would complete it as I fathered my son.

One night, we told my father that our baby was a boy.

Dad smiled and nodded his head. "John, having a son of your own is going to be one of the best things that's ever happened *to* you and *for* you," he said. "And do you realize that this baby will be the first of my grandchildren to carry on our family name?"

Everyone was wonderfully encouraging, and little by little, my confidence increased. I thought about my nephews and how much I enjoyed them. They loved me, too, and had no problem relating to me. And when I told our pastor, he simply said, "I think it's fantastic! I've seen you around little boys, and you're wonderful with them. I can't imagine anyone being a better dad than you. Your son will be blessed having you for a father."

Anne and I had lots of shopping to do during those months, now that we were convinced there would, after all, be a baby in our home. First of all, she was quickly outgrowing her clothes. Late that summer, when Anne had about four more months to go, my mom and her husband, Tom, came to visit us from Ohio, and they took us to Seattle for a weekend. While we were there, they took us to an expensive maternity store.

"I'd like to buy you a new outfit, Anne," Tom said. "I can only afford one, so keep trying them on until you find the one you like best."

Anne tried on one outfit after another, and we applauded every time she emerged from the dressing room. The store's selection was first-rate, and nothing looked anything short of terrific on her.

"I can't decide," Anne told me after nearly an hour of trying things on.

"It's up to you," I replied. "They all look fantastic to me."

After much deliberation, Anne eliminated all but 15 outfits.

Tom nodded and instructed, "Okay, now pick your top 10 and rate them in order."

Anne complied and left Tom with her top-10 list of maternity outfits. He stayed behind to pay for the one she had rated best, and the rest of us headed for the car. Anne and I felt deeply thankful that Tom so generously wanted to get her such a nice gift. Later that day, however, when we looked in the trunk, we found not one outfit but bags and bags of maternity clothes. Tom had bought Anne all 10 of her favorite outfits!

We were shocked and felt incredibly honored. "I feel like a princess!" Anne told him, giving him a bear hug.

Tom just grinned and enjoyed how much pleasure he had been able to provide.

As for my shopping, I felt a strong sense that I should purchase some "boy" things for the baby. I bought a football, a soccer ball, and a basketball—the very things that had represented fear, failure, and rejection to me. And deep inside, I experienced a certain amount of healing as I bought them. Now they represented something amazing and exciting: a joyful future to be shared with a healthy son. Somewhere during those months, I remember thinking, *I'm so glad God gives us nine months of pregnancy so we can contemplate this great responsibility of raising a child.*

We had no idea at first what to name our boy, but we felt extremely grateful to Dr. Stewart, who had been such a help and encouragement to us through so much. His first name was Timothy. We liked the way that could be shortened to Tim or Timmy. When we looked up the name in a book, it gave the meaning as "one who honors the Lord." We really appreciated that, and so we finally decided it would be a good name for our son and asked Dr. Stewart if he would mind our using it.

"I'd love it!" he responded enthusiastically.

We also liked the name Edward, so that became Timmy's middle name.

Anne and I continued to pray together about our baby and our family's future. She, of course, continually prayed for a healthy, happy boy who would weather the childbirth process and grow healthy and strong.

As time went by, I prayed often, *God please help me to be a good father to our son, a good role model.* Because of my experience, I was concerned that Timmy might reject me in his teen years. The more I thought about it, though, the more I realized that if I expressed my affection regularly and clearly, Timmy would not reject me but would return my love. So, anxious but trusting God, we continued to pray that He would help us to be the best parents possible.

Anne Before long, I was as big as a house. The baby was sticking out so far that whenever I taught a computer training class, someone would say, "Anne, why don't you sit down to teach us? I'm afraid you're going to deliver right now!"

Those last months of pregnancy were among the most fulfilling times of my life. As a mother-to-be, I joined an informal sorority of women who had already had babies and wanted to share their joys with me. This aspect of being a woman and of bonding with other women was something I could not have imagined in my past life. It was so good and right and pure, and I felt welcome in the world in a way I never had before.

Part of the sorority "program" involved parties, of course—baby showers. Friends, family, and co-workers gave me three showers in November and December, with good food and great fun. Among the many presents were Winnie the Pooh classic clothes and accessories to go with all the Pooh nursery decorations John and his parents put up. Our two families then furnished the room with everything a baby could need.

We weren't sure how we would make it on one income after the birth—a ministry income at that—but we knew we wanted me to stay home and raise our son. And since God had provided so generously for all our needs so far, we were confident that His faithfulness would continue.

But now another concern arose. Timmy was in a breach position, and he wouldn't turn on his own. At eight months, then at nine months, this child would not flip over and put his head down. Dr. Stewart did one last ultrasound, wondering if there was some way he could turn the baby. "No," he told me as he studied the screen, "the placenta is in the wrong place. I think we'd better plan on a Cesarean delivery."

That night, John and I picked the date for Timmy's birth. We checked the calendar, and the next day we called the doctor's office. "We'd like to schedule our C-section for December 17," we said.

John Early on December 17, 1996, Anne got up feeling both excited and apprehensive. We had packed our bags the night before, and now we hurried out of bed, washed our faces, pulled on our clothes, and headed for St. Vincent's Hospital.

"John, is this really happening?" Anne asked as we drove.

"It's really happening, Anne," I assured her. "The suspense is about to end. It's our baby's birthday!"

"I can't believe it," she said, placing her hand on her swollen tummy and closing her eyes.

The birthing suite was elegant and well appointed, and its attractive furnishings conveyed a sense of well-being. We settled in and tried to be as relaxed as possible. We prayed together, talked to the various medical people who came and went, and waited. After the usual preparations, Anne was given an epidural block, and before long she was wheeled into the delivery room. We said another quick prayer together.

Would everything be all right? Neither of us asked the question, but we both felt it lurking in the backs of our minds. After two miscarriages, we were braced for the worst while continuing to believe God for the best.

At about 7:30 A.M., Anne went into surgery, and I was able to be at her side. Less than half an hour later, our baby was born, and to our great comfort, his birth was without complications. He hadn't yet been lifted out of Anne's body when we heard him cry for the first time.

What a miracle! The mysterious little person who had been hiding inside Anne's body had suddenly appeared. After all the challenges along the way, Timmy Paulk was alive and well. We could count 10 toes and 10 fingers, and we found ourselves studying a face that looked vaguely familiar, a little like a combination of his daddy's and his grandma's.

While we both began to cry tears of gratitude and relief, Timothy Edward Paulk screamed in rage as his little body was cleaned, weighed, and wrapped. The pediatric nurse grinned at the sound of his hearty voice. "Eight pounds, one ounce," she announced. "Twenty inches. You've got a beautiful son."

At long last, our first child had come into the world. Our dream of being parents had come true. Our prayers had finally been answered.

Anne

My whole body was draped with medical paraphernalia, and I was connected to all sorts of IVs. Because of my anesthesia, I could hardly move anything except my head. But when I heard Timmy's cry, I looked over at John, who was sitting beside me. I started sobbing and said, "Honey, we have a baby!" We both began to cry tears of incredible joy.

I didn't care that they were now sewing up my stomach, and fortunately I couldn't feel a thing anyway. Our happiness was overwhelming. Once the suturing was complete, John and I held Timmy, hardly able to believe our eyes. I can't express the awe I felt at being a mother and at the privilege of being given the opportunity to raise a child of my own. Timmy's birth made me aware of God's sovereignty in a deeper way. If God intends for somebody to make it through the pregnancy process and be born on this earth, it will happen. It was by His design that we're all here, including John, Anne, and Timmy Paulk.

John The weeks that followed Timmy's birth blur in my memory. We had so many visitors—both friends and family who were nearly as blessed by the birth of our son as we were. We took turns caring for him—feeding him, changing him, getting up at night to look after him. And it was during this time that I believe God gave me a new vision for my life—for all our lives.

I was rocking Timmy on my chest one night when I felt myself drift away. Suddenly I saw Anne and myself many years in the future—I knew that because we were obviously much older, with age spots and wrinkles on our hands. We were backstage in some well-used theater; the wooden planks of the stage were peeling and worn. From the back we saw a man standing at a podium; from that angle he reminded me of a young Franklin Graham. As I glanced into the crowd, I saw that every seat was filled.

The man started to speak. "Ladies and gentlemen," he said, "I'm here tonight to bear witness to the truth that homosexuality can be overcome. My own parents were once homosexuals but were transformed by God. And not only have my parents left homosexuality, but so have thousands of others. I'm living proof that it can be done!"

After the vision, I tried to understand what it might mean. I wondered if I had imagined the scene, but the tears on my face confirmed the presence of God's Spirit. I believed He had revealed something of the future to me and that Timmy was part of God's great plan to rescue people from the way of life Anne and I had left behind.

This new life Anne and I shared with Timmy was so sacred, so much a gift from God. And in that moment, I could not imagine a better place in all the world than sitting in a rocking chair, holding my firstborn son, and knowing that my loving wife was in the next room, waiting for me.

Anne　In mid-1998, John and I decided to try to have another child. This time I was able to get pregnant after taking my temperature for just a few months. We were astonished when I missed my period and then took a pregnancy test, which showed positive.

I immediately followed up with my gynecologist and heard it again: "Yes, Anne, you're pregnant."

We were referred to a highly recommended obstetrician, and after meeting with him, I put my previous lessons into practice immediately. I began thanking God for each day the baby was in my womb. John and I prayed for the young life inside me, and this time we held off telling anyone I was expecting until several more weeks had passed.

Fortunately, this pregnancy was blissfully uneventful. And once we were sure everything was progressing well, we started to explain things to Timmy, who was two years old.

"You're going to be a *big* brother—there's a baby in Mommy's tummy!" we announced.

One day several months later, John asked Timmy, "What would you like to call your baby brother?"

Without a moment's hesitation, Timmy replied, "Alex," naming his brother after his favorite bear. It's amazing how that name sounded just right.

Looking back, I never thought I would be married, never imagined I would be capable of loving a husband and having such joy in a marriage relationship. I certainly would never have dreamed of experiencing such meaning and delight in the vital job of raising two sons.

John no longer struggles with the fear that he will be rejected by his sons. Timmy adores his daddy, looks up to him, waits eagerly for him to come home at night, and wrestles with him on the floor. They have such a healthy relationship. And, little as he is, I can already see that Alex will share the same closeness to his dad.

One day after Timmy had just turned two, he was playing in the family room. A few minutes before, John had left for work, wearing his tie and carrying his briefcase. Timmy got his little lunch pail out of his play box and said, "This is my brief-case." He put his hat on and said, "Where is my tie?" I went upstairs and got him one of his daddy's ties. He climbed into his little car, which was only slightly bigger than he was, and said, "Bye, Mommy! See you later."

"Where are you going, honey?" I asked.

"To the office," he informed me.

With that, he drove into our living room, pretending he had gone to work just like Daddy. What joy it is for both of us to see that Timmy is modeling himself after John!

Sometimes people ask us if we're afraid one of our little boys will be gay. We have absolute confidence that if anyone is going to be gay, it won't be our sons. Timmy is so secure in himself as a "guy," so accepted as a male. And though Alex is still a baby, he, too, is treasured as a little boy.

As for me, I have a better life than I ever could have dreamed possible. With all the little tantrums of childhood and the normal stresses and strains of marriage, my greatest delight is in being a mother and a wife and in being used by God in whatever way He chooses. I feel completely fulfilled, full of purpose and joy.

How hard was it to turn things around, to move out of homosexuality and into a new life? For me, the pain of going through those miscarriages, losing something John and I really treasured, was infinitely harder than the process of coming out of homosexuality. There's just no comparison.

Changing my orientation was, simply, the right thing to do. It was following God and His ways. The cost was really small. One day when I was addressing a group on the subject, I said, "When we're wrestling with this issue of homosexuality, all we can see is our struggle. All we see is our attraction to members of the same gender. We can't look beyond and see the struggles and difficulties other people are going through and relate to them in compassion. We don't have a bigger world. It's a tiny world. It's a self-centered world."

Now that I'm outside that self-centered world and engaged in the gains and losses other people go through every single day, I realize that people are dealing with so many things that are just as difficult as what I went through. People may say homosexuality is unchangeable, but I have to say that it's not only changeable, but also that there are far more difficult things to deal with in life.

I wouldn't trade one iota of what I have now for what I once experienced. Homosexuality has nothing to offer compared to this life I'm living. Yet I'm grateful to God that I had that past, because I think I have greater joy than most people experience in the simple things of life. The "before and after" contrast is enormous. It makes me treasure John, Timmy, Alex, and our life together all the more.

Afterword

❦

In May 1998, John was offered a position with Focus on the Family as a specialist in homosexual issues. He, Anne, and Timmy packed up once again and moved to Colorado Springs, Colorado.

The summer of that year brought a whole new level of exposure for John and Anne, as Anne's testimony appeared in a full-page advertisement in *The New York Times*. That created a firestorm of controversy, as national media were virtually at their doorstep for nearly six months. They were named as two of the 100 most influential people of the year on homosexual issues, and together they gave more than 200 interviews, ending up on the cover of *Newsweek* magazine in August.

That November, John's mother was diagnosed with terminal lung cancer. After a month-long battle, she died, on Christmas Day, surrounded by her family. During her funeral, five people walked forward to accept Jesus Christ into their lives. Her six short years as a Christian radiated the love for others that God had poured out to her.

On June 29, 1999, Alexander Gillett Paulk became the newest member of the family. Timmy has a whole new role as big brother and marvels at this little person who will soon be tagging along behind him.

As their family grows, God continues to provide John and Anne numerous opportunities to share the good news: Freedom from homosexuality is possible through a relationship with Jesus Christ.

Acknowledgments

No one comes out of homosexuality by himself or herself; it takes a community of loving, supportive people. Along our journey to freedom, many people have helped to shape our lives and guide us to wholeness.

Foremost, we would like to thank James C. Dobson, Ph.D., founder and president of Focus on the Family. Dr. Dobson, you have steadfastly supported the family and continue to direct hurting individuals to Jesus Christ without compromise. Thank you for your belief in and support of us.

To the staff of Focus on the Family: We gratefully thank you for welcoming us into your families, lives, and hearts.

Special love and appreciation are extended to these Focus on the Family staff members and friends:

Gary & Leigh Barkalow
Peter & Mona Brandt
Karen Eaglin
Carrie & Steve Earl
Bob Garner
Lela Gilbert
Phil Hildebrand
Caia Hoskins
Melanie Huffman
Al Janssen
Mark Maddox
Jeff Masching
John McKeever
Mac McQuiston
Tom & Deb Minnery
Diane Passno
Gina Platt

Susie Sanguinetti
Don & Diana Schmierer
Kara Schwab
Amy & Ron Stephens
Amy Tracy
Mike & Nancy Trout
Shane Wagoner
Steve & Candice Watters
Sherri Woods
Leslie Yeaton

To Bob Davies, executive director of Exodus North America: Thank you for your continuous support and encouragement. You are a valuable brother and a steadying force for the ex-gay movement.

To Frank and Anita Worthen: Words cannot express our heart-felt gratitude and love for you. Your wisdom and experience put us on the path toward heterosexuality. Thank you for continuing to help others leave the bondage of homosexuality and see the light of Christ.

To Mike Riley, senior pastor of Church of the Open Door in San Rafael, California: Mike, you are like a father to us. Your door always remains open whenever we need you. Thank you for the numerous hours you spent counseling us while we were stumbling through the dating process. We'll never forget your tears during our wedding ceremony. We love you.

To Mike and Angie Haley: Thank you for your friendship and continued love and support. We would feel lost without you both being here in Colorado.

Thanks are extended to Rebecca Cain who spent hour after hour transcribing cassette tapes.

To the memory of John's mother, Jill Tibbals, who died on Christmas Day, 1998. You were a wonderful mother and grandmother. Your untimely death leaves a void no one will ever fill. We love you.

To our dear sons, Timothy and Alexander: We love and cherish you with all our hearts. We are here for you. We will listen and respond to your needs and cries for help. We will share your triumphs and struggles along the way. We won't be perfect, but we promise to point you toward the One who will always be able to provide for you what we cannot. We're proud of you, Timmy and Alex, and we love watching you grow up. We hope you'll be proud of us.

Most importantly, we thank our Heavenly Father for giving us a life we never thought possible. You are the Father who is always there and never rejects. We love You.

Resources for Additional Help

᠅

Organizations

Exodus International is a worldwide coalition of Christian ministries that offer support to men and women seeking to overcome homosexuality. Many of these ministries have specialized services for family members and friends, including support groups, one-on-one counseling, literature, and other helpful resources.

For a free packet of literature on the work of Exodus, including a complete list of referral ministries, contact Exodus International/North America, P.O. Box 77652, Seattle, WA 98177 (206/784-7799).

National Association for Research and Therapy of Homosexuality (NARTH) is an organization of nearly seven hundred professionals across the country who treat homosexuality from a variety of perspectives. Contact them by writing: NARTH, 1510 Elverand Dr., Thousand Oaks, CA 91362-2129 (818/789-4440).

Books

Many excellent books are available to help you understand and overcome homosexuality. Ask for titles at your local Christian bookstore. If you prefer, you can obtain many of these books by mail. For a free catalog of books on homosexuality and related issues, contact Regeneration Books, P.O. Box 9830, Baltimore, MD 21284 (410/661-0284).

John Paulk is a legislative and cultural affairs analyst with Focus on the Family, specializing in homosexual issues. Among his duties, he leads a national conference called "Love Won Out" for people who care about the growing tragedy of homosexuality in youth. He and Anne address audiences across the nation and have appeared in such national and international media as *People*, *Newsweek*, *Time*, *Rolling Stone*, *60 Minutes*, *Oprah*, *Good Morning America*, *The 700 Club*, and *ABC World News*. John is also the author of *Not Afraid to Change*. To arrange media interviews or speaking engagements, contact the Paulks at:

Focus on the Family
8605 Explorer Drive
Colorado Springs, CO 80920

More Faith-Building Resources From *Focus on the Family* ®

"Amy and Jason: Two True Stories—Exposing the Truth About Gender Identity" *
by Focus on the Family's Youth Culture Department

Coming Out of Homosexuality
by Bob Davies and Lori Rentzel, published by InterVarsity Press

Someone I Love Is Gay
by Anita Worthen and Bob Davies, published by InterVarsity Press

A Strong Delusion
by Joe Dallas, published by Harvest House

"A New Coming Out" *
"Focus on the Family" broadcast audiocassette featuring John and Anne Paulk

"Focus on the Family Position Statement on Homosexual Rights" *

These resources can only be requested by calling Focus on the Family at 1-800-A-FAMILY (1-800-232-6459). Friends in Canada may write Focus on the Family, P.O. Box 9800, Stn. Terminal, Vancouver, B.C. V6B 4G3 or call 1-800-661-9800. To request any of the other items on this page, call Focus on the Family or visit your local Christian bookstore. Visit our Web Site (www.family.org) to learn more about the ministry or find out if there is a Focus on the Family office in your country.

FOCUS ON THE FAMILY®

Welcome to the Family!

Whether you received this book as a gift, borrowed it from
a friend, or purchased it yourself, we're glad you read it! It's just
one of the many helpful, insightful and encouraging
resources produced by Focus on the Family.

In fact, that's what Focus on the Family is all about—providing inspiration, information and biblically based advice to people in all stages of life.

It began in 1977 with the vision of one man, Dr. James Dobson, a licensed psychologist and author of 16 best-selling books on marriage, parenting, and family. Alarmed by the societal, political, and economic pressures that were threatening the existence of the American family, Dr. Dobson founded Focus on the Family with one employee—an assistant— and a once-a-week radio broadcast, aired on only 36 stations.

Now an international organization, Focus on the Family is dedicated to preserving Judeo-Christian values and strengthening the family through more than 70 different ministries, including eight separate daily radio broadcasts; television public service announcements; 11 publications; and a steady series of books and award-winning films and videos for people of all ages and interests.

Recognizing the needs of, as well as the sacrifices and important contribution made by, such diverse groups as educators, physicians, attorneys, crisis pregnancy center staff and single parents, Focus on the Family offers specific outreaches to uphold and minister to these individuals, too. And it's all done for one purpose, and one purpose only: to encourage and strengthen individuals and families through the life-changing message of Jesus Christ.

●   ●   ●

For more information about the ministry, or if we can be of help to your family, simply write to Focus on the Family, Colorado Springs, CO 80995 or call 1-800-A-FAMILY (1-800-232-6459). Friends in Canada may write Focus on the Family, P.O. Box 9800, Stn. Terminal, Vancouver, B.C. V6B 4G3 or call 1-800-661-9800. Visit our Web site—www.family.org— to learn more about the ministry or to find out if there is a Focus on the Family office in your country.

We'd love to hear from you!